Praise for Fir€

"I've created content online for nearly a decade and this is the book I wish I had at the start of my journey! The online world can be quite critical but in her uniquely empathetic way, Jillian cuts through the noise of what I've learned the hard way through much frustration and hours of lost sleep ruminating on 'the perfect response' to the trolls and haters.

Jillian's concept of "You make a thing; you make the rules" is worth buying this book for—it's a game changer."
>—Brad Barrett, Co-host and co-founder
>of the ChooseFI Podcast

"This book is about so much more than the challenges we face with our external critics. It's about confronting your inner critic with self-compassion. And creating emotional boundaries with yourself, so that you can create content in ways that feel positive and authentic for you. When you show up as your true self, the world will meet you there."
>—Cait Flanders, author of *The Year of Less*
>and *Adventures in Opting Out*

"As someone who has received plenty of online hate—and constantly gets asked how to deal with it—I will now send folks to Jillian's book. Thoughtful, empathetic, and full of actionable information. A great read for any online creator."
>—Tori Dunlap, creator of Her First 100k

"Legendary boxer Mike Tyson famously said "Everybody has a plan until they get punched in the mouth." And creating online is a lot like getting punched in the mouth, repeatedly. When I first started publishing online I thought I had a plan for this criticism, but found out quickly how much those punches hurt. I desperately wish I would have had this book back then. If you create content on the internet, this book is a must read for knowing how to handle the inevitable punches coming your way."
>—Nick True, creator of Mapped Out Money

"Never read the comments" is the advice veteran content creators share with their newer counterparts. It's great advice, but what do you do if you've already read them? Jillian shares how to expertly handle online criticism in this must-read book for any online content creator. From the What If's to the anonymous trolls to the comments from friends and family, Jillian shares how to ignore these distractors so you can concentrate on what YOU do best—create awesome content!

—Mindy Jenson Bigger Pocket Money Podcast
co-host and author

"The internet isn't just a collection of hilarious memes, selfies and hot-takes. It's also a place where ideas are spread, communities are formed and millions of transactions are processed daily. For this to happen, we need entrepreneurs, writers and creatives to have the confidence and clarity needed to share their innermost thoughts with the world. In *Fire the Haters*, Jillian doesn't just offer a heaping dose of encouragement, she provides thoughtful guidance on what to expect before and after you press publish."

—Julien Saunders, rich & REGULAR, writer,
speaker and digital entrepreneur

"Every worthy idea, innovation, and creative work draws vitriol and critics—and those trolls create a huge emotional drain. As creatives, we're told to 'toughen up' or 'develop thick skin,' but how? If you find yourself shrinking in order to people-please, you must read Jillian's honest and heartfelt book."

—Paula Pant, host of the Afford Anything podcast

"If you want to be a creator, entrepreneur, or public figure, at some point you will encounter haters. There are two ways to deal with this. One: throw up your hands and quit. Two: read this book and learn how to 'fire the haters'. Having overcome poverty, dyslexia, and online hate, Jillian teaches you how to deal with haters in a compassionate, empathetic voice and gives you practical tips that are easy to follow. Reading her book is like reading advice from a best friend or a sister and it will give you the courage to push through criticism so you can get back to what matters the most—your most creative, authentic work."

—Kristy Shen, author of *Quit Like a Millionaire*

"Haters suck. But giving up on your dreams sucks more. Don't let the haters win! Pick up this book and let Jillian help guide you through this beautifully messy place they call The Internet. It'll be like having coffee with your best friend, only a best friend who also happens to know exactly what you need to succeed online."

—J. Money, AllStarMoney

"Jillian has proven, yet again, why her work is so powerful for so many of us. She isn't afraid to tell the truth—whether it is a list of concrete ideas on how we can get out of our own way or bravely sharing the struggles she met along her path—and she does it with compassion and humor on every page. While her intention may have been to simply provide a guidebook for a healthy, creative life online, these truths extend well beyond the comment section of a social media account and into the real lives of the humans behind the screen."

—August Cabrera, Writer

"As a creator and entrepreneur in the internet age, we walk a fine line between professional success and personal boundaries—not to mention feelings of imposter syndrome, fear and self-doubt. Jillian offers a framework for managing those feelings without cutting ourselves off from our creativity and our unique capacity to innovate, so we can still leverage all of our inimitable talent while protecting ourselves from overexposure and burnout."

—Stefanie O'Connell Online Entrepreneur and Influencer

"Everyone who dares to put their thoughts, heart and soul "out there" for all to see ultimately risks rejection and criticism of their work. Many also have to fight even more daunting battles against their inner critic, or suffer from imposter syndrome.

Like that supportive friend or mentor who has clearly been there herself, Jillian Johnsrud brings a refreshing perspective and an arsenal of practical strategies that enable us to overcome the fear and resistance that often accompanies putting our best creative efforts out into the world."

—Dr. Peter Gallant, Professor and Writer

"Fire The Haters: Finding Courage to Create Online in a Critical World is a book I so wish I had when I started my online journey. It would have saved me so much time and heartache. Jillian Johnsrud has written the definitive guide to coping with being a content creator in today's fast-paced and often inhumane virtual world. A must read for not only the modern digital entrepreneur but just about anyone who creates online."

—Doc G. Host of Earn & Invest Podcast

FINDING THE COURAGE TO CREATE
ONLINE IN A CRITICAL WORLD

FIRE
THE
HATERS

JILLIAN JOHNSRUD

ISBN:
978-1-7365498-1-0 (Paperback)
978-1-7365498-2-7 (Hardcover)
978-1-7365498-0-3 (eBook)

Library of Congress Control Number: 2021940296

All content reflects our opinion at a given time and can change as time progresses. All information should be taken as an opinion and should not be misconstrued for professional or legal advice. The contents of this book are informational in nature and are not legal or tax advice, and the authors and publishers are not engaged in the provision of legal, tax, or any other advice.

Front cover image by 100Covers
Book Design by FormattedBooks

Printed by Jillian Johnsrud in the United States of America.

First printing edition 2021.

P.O. Box 335
Kalispell, Mt 59903

www.jillianjohnsrud.com

Dedication

To my husband, Adam, who is relentlessly dedicated to making all my dreams a possibility.

To my coaching clients who laid bare every challenge and fear with courage and vulnerability, allowing me to discover the solutions.

To my incredible audience across email and social media for their continued kindness, friendship and support.

Contents

Introduction

"A ship in harbor is safe—but that is not what ships are built for."
—John A. Shedd

I was a few months into blogging about personal finance, when a big curation website agreed to publish one of my pieces. The idea of seeing my work on a site I respected was thrilling. I was new to writing about money: bright-eyed, and full of optimism. In my naivety, I couldn't see any downside to this opportunity.

Three days after my article was published, I almost quit writing forever.

There were a few things I didn't know at the time. First, titles aren't typically written by the author. Big sites and news outlets often change the title of your work to something more catchy, or inflammatory to serve as clickbait. Rage reading is better than no one reading when publishing sites are playing a numbers game.

The second thing I learned about these sites is that their readers have no loyalty or grace for you, the unknown author. I had always written on my own websites to my friendly audience. Occasionally a wave of new readers would show up and I would receive some negative feedback. But my website was my online home. A friendly and safe corner of the Internet where I could interact with people who enjoyed my work.

I'm not sure if anyone even read my article on the curation site. It was as if the title alone outraged them, and they headed straight to the comments section to let loose on me.

Three days into this shit storm, I emailed a fellow blogger J. Money.

"How do you handle this? I'm binge eating. I can't sleep. I wake up in the middle of the night with my mind racing with rebuttals

and defenses. I'm trying to explain myself in the comments but it's only getting worse. I don't think I'm cut out for the creative life. This is brutal. I might quit writing."

Jay said, *"Oh, sweetie. You never read the comments. Ever."*
My first thought was, *"Wait? That's an option?"*
He said that he never looks at the comments when he writes for big news outlets. Occasionally his friends will look, but they are under strict orders not to tell him what the comments say.

Instead, I handled it entirely wrong: I defended my ideas, my story, my intent, and my personal life from vicious attacks and misinterpretations. As a result, I almost quit.

Because I didn't understand how to cope with online criticism, trolls and haters. I made every mistake. I assumed how I interacted with friends and family would transfer directly to this online life. That incorrect assumption almost stopped me before I even had a chance to get going.

The lesson here? What works in your daily personal life isn't going to work online. You need to learn a whole new perspective, a new set of rules and develop a different understanding of how to interact online.

The Internet Got Mean

In the late 90's about the time the U.S. Military opted to become "Kinder and Gentler," the Internet decided to go in the opposite direction.

The early Internet seemed as sweet as a 90's after-school sitcom. We were buying and selling Beanie Babies on eBay, finding love in chat rooms and my grandmother learned to send e-cards for every imaginable holiday. And those forwarded email chains! Sweet, encouraging stories, or superstitions of luck... as long as you forwarded to ten people.

Then the Internet got mean.

This unprecedented opportunity to start a business or find an audience for projects was being born, while the Internet became darker.

People found an anonymous outlet to vent their frustrations and anger. They became more demanding, negative and extreme. Social media networks struggled (and failed) to keep platforms free of hate, threats, and constant bullying.

Even friends and family showed off their more extreme and cruel sides with less consideration or grace given for our differences.

One of the struggles in creating things and sharing them online, is that most online things are less than a generation old. We didn't watch our parents acting reasonably in Facebook groups or teaching us how to respectfully comment on Instagram posts. Our parents might have had dozens of opportunities to teach us how to behave at a friend's home, answer the phone respectfully or how to accept a sports loss with grace. No one taught us how to act online; instead, it became the inexperienced leading the naive.

This book will be your field guide—a survival manual to help navigate the often scary process of creating your best work and sharing it online in a world of so much criticism. My goal is to help you survive and even thrive in these exciting, yet dangerous waters.

Essential Yet Seemingly Dangerous

When I talk to creatives, small business owners, and entrepreneurs they are amazed and excited about the power of the Internet to help them find and connect with customers or audiences.

But at the same time, almost everyone wishes they could quit the Internet at some point. The Internet is like encountering a lion, incredible, but dangerous.

What we create differs vastly. We share it online in a dozen different mediums. You might be a Writer, Social Media Influencer, Coach, Service Provider, Artist, Entrepreneur, Thought Leader, Podcaster, Musician, Real Estate Investor, Consultant, Athlete, YouTuber, Restaurant Owner, Speaker, Non-Profit, Actor, Blogger, Politician, or Small Business Owner promoting your offering online, or in hundreds of other similar roles!

We all have this in common: we create things and hope the Internet can help us find the ideal customers for our work, those for whom our creative and entrepreneurial work truly resonates. The Internet made the table longer, removed gatekeepers, and gave us reach around the globe.

Navigating Three Challenges

Chatting with creatives and entrepreneurs is just about my favorite thing in the world. So I organized this book like our conversation would flow. If we went out for coffee and chatted about your concerns about growing your business, this is the advice I'd give you.

We would chat about the three types of challenges you face: online criticism, the inner critic, and fear of failure. I'd help you develop best practices to keep you and your work productive.

Part 1: Fire the Haters: Overcoming Online Criticism

The Internet is becoming a more cruel and ill-mannered place. You need to learn to navigate these haters and other bad actors. If you haven't experienced this online hate yet, you will. I promise. Either because you became bolder and created something even more special and interesting or because more people are paying attention to the things that you create. (Both of which are good things!)

You'll also need to learn how to create boundaries with your work—emotional boundaries. So you don't mistake your work for yourself. It's not—you are not your work. You'll learn how to create rules around your work and your online presence that keeps you sane. And how to clearly and consistently communicate those rules to your team, audience, and customers.

Part 2: Overcoming Imposter Syndrome and the Inner Critic

Imposter syndrome strikes us at every level. Want to get started? Imposter syndrome. Want to go bigger, grow into new areas and try new things? Imposter syndrome. It's the critical inner voice that dishes out criticism and knows exactly where to hit you at your most vulnerable points.

This is the "messy middle" where your skill doesn't match your taste, just yet. The place where you aren't the most experty expert, so how can you be confident in what you offer when others are clearly better than you? This is the stage where your favorite form of procrastination is preparation.

Part 3: Failure, Fear, Then Finding the Courage to Share Your Best Work

"What if it doesn't work?"
"What if I fail?"
"What if no one buys it?"
"What if I lose?"
"What if I'm a failure?"
"What if I can't recover?"

This is especially challenging for the people pleasers and perfectionists like myself. Because occasionally you will fail, at least a little bit. It's part of playing this game. But failure doesn't have to mean quitting or getting crushed, you can "fail well." You'll learn how to optimize for not quitting. You can create emotional boundaries around your outcomes, win or lose. And learn how to anchor your identity in safer harbors.

By the end of our coffee date, you'll be able to fire the haters, overcome imposter syndrome and your inner critic, then courageously create and share your best work online despite these choppy waters of the Internet.

Risk of Seeking Safety

That first round of negative comments about my blog post on the curation site were brutal. I did everything wrong, so instead of brushing the dust off, I had to nurse my wounds for days. And I almost gave up writing.

There's a reason I never pursued a career in rodeo bull riding; the life of broken ribs isn't for me. I was caught off guard by how risky this seemingly safe creative life was going to be. Sitting at my desk and slowly crafting words into ideas and stories seemed like an incredibly safe pursuit until it wasn't.

Creating your best work and sharing it with the world isn't safe. Not even close. Until you learn to navigate it, it can be choppy waters—full of things that feel dangerous and risky.

First, I want to share the rookie mistakes—the main ways you might try to make this online world feel safer, but instead risk not producing your truly best work in the process.

Play it safe. Your work is more guarded, compromised, less vulnerable, less self-disclosing, and ultimately less honest. You hold back, resisting the ideas or work that really stirs you, and you start creating things that no one would ever take issue with because they are simply too boring for people to notice, let alone care about. Bland is safe.

This pattern irritates me the most because it's the one I can fall into frequently. It's easy to mold yourself into a safer but more mediocre version of what you are capable of. To soften the edges and sand them out. To make the messages more palatable for the masses. In an attempt to make everyone happy, it turns out that no one is engaged or interested.

Slowing down. You create less often (always with very good and rational reasons.) Or you create, but you don't publish and share with the world. New designs, new ideas, new offers are tinkered with behind the scenes in safety. Every new product and new idea has to be perfect, hoping that *"perfect"* will give you a safe harbor or some sort of free pass from criticism or failure.

The slow pace might become like the movement of a glacier, undetectable to the naked eye. Sometimes people will start telling me about their small business idea, dream or creative project that they have been thinking about starting. It all sounds great and I start getting excited about seeing this thing happen.

I'll ask *"How soon until you think you'll start."*

"Oh, I don't know," they will say. *"I've been thinking about it for years."*

Years!?! I mean, I get it. I've let imposter syndrome and fear of failure hold me hostage for far too long on projects. But you're not playing it safe by not playing the game. Sitting out simply guarantees you won't win.

Detour. You get busy with other projects or work. You take up new interests. Because in all the hustle and bustle, you don't have to own up to yourself or others that you are avoiding your real work of creating. Systems and processes are a great detour.

Whenever I am really hesitant about a creative project, a home task suddenly feels dramatically urgent. A friend will ask how the project is coming along. *"It's going great! Right now, I have to finish up (cleaning out my closets, organizing my office, buying school supplies for the kids) before I can really dive in. But just as soon as that's taken care of, I'll really be able to focus."*

Many creatives become *"project completion machines"* for any project except finishing what matters most.

Hiding. Maybe you created a new service, offer, product or piece of content. Maybe you even hit publish on the website, uploaded it to YouTube, or emailed it out to your list. But then you retreat. You hide. Instead of talking about it everywhere, instead of continuing to promote your work, instead of trying to get people to see it, you take your foot off the gas. You coast. All the work went into creating and very little effort is made sharing that work. Because it's in the sharing that we feel vulnerable.

Staying small. Maybe you aren't doing any of the things described above. You're creating, sharing, promoting to your audience, you're focused and moving quickly, you're showing up as your biggest, best and most authentic self.

The only problem is that you're staying small. With your long standing customers and audience, in your tiny corner of the Internet, to warm and friendly crowds, you're staying in familiar and comfortable spaces online.

You do the things you've always done. Same songs, same roles, same recipes, same offers, same services, same products. Because they work. There's little risk of criticism or failure. No need to wrestle with imposter syndrome all over again. It's comfortable.

You don't seek out anything bigger because you know that a wave of new attention will bring a wave of new criticism or failure. Even when opportunity lands in your lap, you resist and hesitate.

In his book *Greenlights*, Matthew McConaughey shares the point in his career that he stopped accepting romantic comedy roles. He had an amazing career as the romantic lead in big movies like *How to Lose a Guy in 10 Days* and *Failure to Launch*. It was a risk and a gamble to reject the thing that was working. It's scary to leave safe harbors. But we would have never gotten the incredible movies he has made since if he hadn't taken that leap.

There's only two options. You figure out how to navigate sharing your work online or you don't.

And the people who don't either stay small, go slow, hide, or quit.

Just like I almost quit.

Toni Morrison once said, *"If there's a book that you want to read, but it hasn't been written yet, then you must write it."* So here I go. This is the book I wish I had those first few years. It's all the cheat codes from everyone who has gone before you and figured it out. I've gathered the collective wisdom from creatives and entrepreneurs of every stripe.

How do we navigate the Internet in a way that keeps us sane, healthy, and productive? How do we make sure our imposter syndrome or fear of public failure don't take us out of the game? How do we navigate this incredible, yet dangerous place so we can do work that matters to us?

Just because something is scary doesn't mean it has to be dangerous. This book will teach you to navigate new places, new projects and bigger audiences. By the end you'll know how to manage and fire the online haters and trolls. You'll know how to create clear rules around your time, energy and your work, and communicate that to your team and audience. You'll get tools to handle criticism and lack of encouragement from family and friends. You'll develop a new perspective about staying in the game and committing to the process of your work, even though the outcomes aren't where you want them to be, just yet.

You can fire the haters and find the courage to create online in a critical world.

PART 1

Dealing with Online Critics: Fire the Haters

Most creators, entrepreneurs and public figures don't need the entire world to love their work. You understand that tastes differ. If you write romance novels, you know that some people prefer cookbooks. Some people will always vote for their party line or only purchase jazz music.

What we fear are the Bad Actors; the ill-intentioned, mean, or ill-tempered person. Merriam-Webster describes Bad Actors as *"unruly, turbulent, or contentious individuals"*. On the Internet we call them haters.

Bad actors aren't people who care about you and your work. They won't give you thoughtful and helpful feedback.

Instead, these bad actors seem to spend their free time roaming the Internet, seeing who they can humiliate, shame, bully, or harass today. Perhaps it's a sport for them, or just an outflowing of their temperament and character.

My creative life would have been a very short one if I hadn't been able to name these bad actors as such, freeing me up to move on with my creative and entrepreneurial work. The more I have learned about their motivations, triggers, and outbursts, the easier it has become to name the bad actors when I see them in action.

In order to survive and thrive in the online world, you have to learn how to create rules and systems around your work that keep you sane, healthy and productive. You'll have to be very clear about the rules because the Internet doesn't have the same sensibilities as you do.

Soon you'll be able to fire the haters and understand their behavior says more about them than it does you.

CEO of the Internet

"Isn't it amazing that the people who have the least
to offer you also have the most demands?"
—Unknown

Have you met the CEO of the Internet? It's the person who is convinced that they run the online world. Asserting their position as CEO, they attempt to fire, reprimand, demote or control you, their low-level employee. Perhaps you spoke out of turn or created something they don't care for, or maybe your work simply doesn't live up to the CEO of the Internet's standards. Like all good CEOs and leaders, they threaten to fire you via Twitter or in the comment section.

In reality, the CEO of the Internet has a cushy job. They want all the power and none of the responsibility or risk of creating any work themselves. They cruise around the Internet, seeing who they want to demote, fire or humiliate today—never needing to do any of the hard creative work of actually making things.

Except they aren't your boss. And boy, does that irk them.

The CEO of the Internet only has the power that you alone give him and that makes his blood boil.

So they will rage and YELL IN ALL CAPS. They will huff and puff. They will try to bully you into acknowledging or accepting the power and attention that they crave: to get their own way.

The CEO of the Internet doesn't need to run the entire Internet. Instead, they specialize in their interest, subject, religious issue, particular taste, physical appearance, or—the ones I attract the most—the CEO of spelling and grammar.

In the early days of writing, I couldn't afford an editor. My writing was filled with simple typos and spelling errors. I've lost count of the number of comments left by the CEOs of spelling and grammar.

"You shouldn't be allowed to write."

"You can't be a serious writer without knowing how to spell."

"Hire an editor or stop wasting our time."

"You're ruining the English language."

The CEO of the Internet is like the Wizard of Oz. She tries to seem all knowing and all powerful. But it's just smoke and mirrors. She only has the power you choose to give her.

She will demand that your work exactly fits her taste. Your style should match her own. You should only be allowed to talk about the things she finds appropriate. Veer off topic and she will blast you.

Your physical shape and size should be exactly to his liking or else he will deem you worthless. Your tone should be his preference or else he'll accuse you of being shrill or annoying.

The CEO of the Internet stands on many different soap boxes. But they have a common attribute: they will act like it's their full-time job to keep everyone in line. Towing their line. Living up to their demanding standards. And if you step outside, they will exert all the force they can to either get you back in line or push you out of the circle.

Fire the CEO of the Internet

She's the school bully. But she isn't the CEO of *your* work.

Feel free to tell the CEO, *"Actually, you're not my boss. You have no say over my work. In fact, your opinion has zero impact on my job security because I was never working for you. You can show yourself out now."* Practice that a few times. You feel free to say it out loud or give written instructions. Then you can get back to work.

"But, Jillian, isn't editing a good suggestion?!? Spelling is helpful for the reader's experience."

Sure. And your fans, friends, and employees can give honest and helpful feedback. But let each person do their own job. Let editors be editors. Internet strangers never get to be the CEO of you or your work. Don't give a stranger this power over you.

Don't let the CEO of the Internet bully, harass, or shame you into giving them the power they seek, which is to control you and your work. Fire the CEO of the Internet, keep your friends.

Fake Royalty

The CEO of the Internet is almost always an Internet stranger, and only occasionally a fan. Rarely are other creators childish or petty enough to pretend to be your boss and order you around on Twitter. Because they are busy doing their own work. They have skin in the game. And no time to waste playing bully to other people doing the work.

Except—and this is a big exception—occasionally one person who works in your arena will decide that this little part of the Internet is their kingdom and everyone who resides in that area their subjects. They have anointed themselves king or queen. They act like fake royalty.

Fake royalty writes all laws and makes all sorts of arbitrary decrees, which must be held in the highest regard. This royalty is ruthless. The punishment for crossing them is extreme. In their thirst for power, they will try to turn the rest of their kingdom against you. Because if people realized their alleged power is all smoke and mirrors, the whole construct would fall apart.

My advice, keep being your own awesome self. Perhaps the fake royalty will grow out of their immature games. Or eventually other people in your niche will realize that this fake royalty is simply insecure and power hungry.

Boundaries are a Fence not a Prison

As they say, *"good fences make for good neighbours"*.

You'll need to create rules that serve as a fence around the things you create. Rules are clear boundaries as to what is allowed in and what is kept outside. They are a fence to protect you and your work, not a prison for the audience. You're not holding anyone captive against their will. They are free to go whenever they like, for whatever reason they want. So don't feel bad about building the fence around your work.

Maybe leaving is the hater's last ditch effort of control and manipulation. Perhaps they are leaving because your work isn't to their taste or liking. Either way is fine.

Sometimes my friend Tori Dunlap will post screenshots of people angrily announcing in the comments they are unfollowing her because something isn't exactly to their taste. Her response reads: *This isn't an airport. You don't need to announce your departure.*

SUMMARY:

- The CEO of the Internet wants all the power and none of the risk or hard work of creating.
- The CEO of the Internet isn't your boss and only has the power you give him (or her).
- Take feedback from friends, professionals, and colleagues, not random Internet bullies.
- Fake Royalty tries to run their whole little niche of the Internet. But they are often insecure, immature and power hungry.
- Your boundaries are a fence to protect you and your work—not a prison. The CEO of the Internet can show herself out.

Dumbass Whisperer

"I can't fix all the stupidity on the internet, I'm not the dumbass whisperer."
—Chris Brogan

One morning in 2010, Pat Flynn, creator of the site *Smart Passive Income*, woke up to emails from his entrepreneur friends. They were warning him about an extremely critical comment about Pat that was posted on their websites. This same comment appeared on his site as well. In fact, the commentator had copy and pasted this hateful and cruel comment on dozens if not a hundred websites and message boards.

This wasn't a simply troll who spews random hate. This was a dumbass.

The dumbass will persist in misunderstanding you. They will continue to interpret your intentions, your work, your offer or your service in the wrong way. They will skew the information and draw the wrong conclusion. Over and over. The dumbass will pull you into a fight but never allow their mind to be changed—because they have no desire to learn, grow, or understand.

The only reason they show up to the fight is to vent their anger and stroke their ego through bullying, name calling, and meanness. It doesn't matter that their argument doesn't hold water, isn't logical or even accurate, the only goal is to make you feel stupid, miserable or cause you to give up. If the dumbass can do that, they feel like they have won.

Pat went quiet online. Stopped creating. Stopped posting. This random dumbass caused Pat to question himself and his work. Pat has gone on to help millions of people build businesses. But one dumbass's comment derailed him, thankfully only temporarily.

The Chris Brogan quote that opened this chapter helped set me free. Fixing stupidity isn't your job. Even when the stupidity is surrounding your work or life. It's not your job to force dumbasses to understand your perspective, your intent, your product, or your work, when the dumbass persists—often intentionally—in misunderstanding you.

The trouble with being a dumbass whisperer is that by definition, you are dealing with a dumbass. My great-grandpa raised donkey's (where we get the term ass.) They are a fantastic combination of acting incredibly stubborn and disliking change. They are useful pack animals because if you can get them started, they will persistently continue on a given path.

I'm all for giving people space to grow, change, and learn. But let's be honest, the dumbass isn't looking to change. Like an ass, they are digging in the hooves in their poorly reasoned, cruel and unhelpful ideas with no intention of changing course.

The dumbass who harassed Pat had even more nefarious intent. The reason he persisted in misunderstanding? He was hoping to drive traffic to his own website by gaining attention from his hateful comment—to build himself up by tearing somebody else down. All that hurt was caused for a publicity stunt. The incredible irony is that this dumbass tried to take down the very person who could have helped him grow his business the most.

It's not your job to try to change the dumbass. It's not your job because you have chosen another job already—a far more important one. You chose creative work, idea work, entrepreneur work, hopefully, life-changing or joy-giving work. If you take on a part-time gig as a dumbass whisper, it will only steal away time and energy from your real job.

SUMMARY

- The dumbass will persist in misunderstanding your intentions, work, offer, or service.
- It doesn't matter to the dumbass that their argument doesn't hold logic and isn't even accurate.
- Fixing stupidity on the internet isn't your job. Because you have chosen creative and entrepreneurial work. Let the dumbass misunderstand you and not steal a moment of your time or energy.

Trolls

"Trolls are like seagulls, they swoop in, shit on you, then leave."
—Ryan Nicodemus

A friend of mine mentioned he had a work buddy who spent half an hour every morning before work trolling the Internet leaving hateful comments on random websites and message boards. It was a hobby—his own bizarre way to start the day.

This is such a sad image in my mind. A middle-aged man at his computer looking for people to criticize, tear down, and shame online. Not creating anything, producing anything, or building relationships. His only boost of confidence or worth was in his ability to hurt others. Intentionally causing pain to the creatives and doers of the world is what brought him joy. I started to think trolls might have sociopathic tendencies.

Perhaps, trolls understand they can't use unfiltered hate, shame, and cruelty in their personal relationships or at work because there can be consequences in these environments. But they have this undercurrent of rage with no outlet. Enter the Internet. Now these haters get to dress up like trolls and spew all their anger and frustration at life on you and your work. Better yet, they get to be anonymous so they will never experience any accountability for such bad behavior.

I think morning routines are powerful. And this guy picked about the most pathetic and destructive one imaginable. I saw trolls in a whole new light after that. Not as scary or mean or powerful but as sad, pathetic people. Not doing anything interesting, creative or inventive. Just complaining and hurting others.

Never take criticism from a sociopath. He's an unqualified creative director.

The world is full of smart, sharp, accomplished people who can give you helpful feedback. But quietly pass by this wretched and miserable creature. Trolls have nothing to offer you.

Trolls for Everyone

One of the more funny yet horribly cruel segments on TV is Jimmy Kimmel's *"Mean Tweets."* Celebrities read the mean Tweets that random people have tagged them in. Half of them are amusing simply because the Tweets aren't clever or funny or smart, only random hate from some person on the Internet. Things like *"Kate Hudson is a dead-eyed trash bag that smells like low tide,"* read on the show by Kate Hudson herself, obviously puzzled over the bizarre nature of the Tweet. Or *"Oh how I loathe Nickelback. P.S. Fu** Wanda Sykes."*

I imagine part of the segment's popularity is the reassurance that we all face the same thing. No matter how beautiful, talented, successful or famous you are, there is someone who will throw random hate at you. Nobody is so perfect that a troll on the Internet won't make them a target.

I also find it oddly comforting seeing the most famous people read these horrible things and then laugh it off. Some troll on the Internet isn't going to stop them from acting, creating, and moving forward. Trolls get no vote on their career, or even their day. I hope one day I can read the worst the Internet says about me on TV and genuinely find it funny.

SUMMARY

- Trolls have an overflow of hate, rage and anger that happens to splash on you.
- Trolls might have sociopathic tendencies, which make them unqualified creative directors for your work.
- There is no one beautiful, talented, successful or perfect enough to avoid trolls. You can't avoid them, but they shouldn't get a vote in your work.

Apple Cart People

*"If you never heal from what hurt you, you'll
bleed on people who didn't cut you."*
—Unknown

A few years ago, I wrote an article for a friend's blog that admittedly was a little bit overly flattering. I had highlighted a number of stories that, when all strung together, made me sound more superhuman than mere mortal. And the comments echoed my exceedingly generous and kind nature. After the first 25 comments that were singing my praise, I thought about throwing in a few flaws just to balance out this narrative I had created.

Until I got to one comment, which started with, *"You are the most selfish human ever. How dare you...."*

My heart raced as my mind slowed. I carefully read the sentence again:

The. Most. Selfish.

Wait, what?!?

This comment was the literal opposite of everyone else's opinion. Everyone might as well have been comparing me to Mother Teresa. But not this woman. She read my life story much differently.

Apple Cart People

I heard Elizabeth Gilbert in an interview refer to someone online who was ranting in the comments that *"she tipped over her apple cart."* The image was a perfect metaphor for a situation I had observed a hundred times working online.

Apple cart people are an unsuspecting form of a bad actor. They can seem pleasant and kind enough. Until you say or do that one thing which triggers them, and then they kick over their whole cart of apples right into your comment section.

Unlike trolls or dumbasses, apple cart people might not have started their day with this intention. But once the cart is spilled, they can create a whole lot of chaos.

Hello, Triggers.

When you create something and ship it into the world it's not entirely yours anymore. Your stories, ideas, and art blend with the thoughts and perspectives of other people. Your work gets mixed with others' stories and experiences. Mixed with their joys, their pain, and their old hurts.

A trigger is created when an old pain or hurt gets pressed by the work you create. An old hurt that was never fully resolved and healed, like an old bruise. If you create enough things and share them with enough people, you will unknowingly trigger some people. It might be things that seem very innocent to you. Birthdays, weddings, babies born, vacations, your stories or even your pricing, success, or new projects.

The comment I received went on with *"How could you abandon your mother? What a horribly selfish daughter."*

My eyes slowly scanned those words, and my mind started to race with how in the world did this reader come to that conclusion. I started frantically creating rebuttals in my mind. I mentally started explaining myself, the situation, and all the facts that she misinterpreted.

But then I paused. She wasn't really commenting on my story or my life. She was commenting on her own. Maybe she was the mother who had been abandoned in her time of need by her children. Maybe she was the child who gave up her own life to help her mother. Either way, her response wasn't about me.

Deep Bruise

Sometimes people don't know they have a trigger. It's like a bruise that has healed on the skin surface. By the looks of it, it's gone. A little brush against it causes no pain. But if someone knows the exact spot to push and applies pressure with their thumb, the pain of the old hurt is evident in the reaction. You can spot a trigger when there is a disproportionate reaction.

An old bruise had been hit. A nerve struck. And people will cry out in pain, fully convinced that you are the sole source of their pain. Otherwise normal, kind people might call you names, swear, and try to fight with you.

Trigger Warnings

If you suspect that your work will trigger people, please give them a warning. Somethings are almost always triggers for people: domestic abuse, crimes against humanity, death, rape, body dysmorphia, and so many others.

Any extremely painful life experience should include a simple *"Trigger Warning"* at the top of an article, social media post or before a video plays. This will give your audience time to choose for themselves if they want to engage with that past pain today which might send their day into a tailspin. These deep bruises can take a lifetime to heal.

Knowing it's not what you created, but how it engages with another's stories and life, I suggest kindness as your response.

Someone might be howling in pain, and this is your chance to show empathy and compassion. We all could use a bit more of both online.

Create a Wide Circle for Your Bruises

Turns out as creatives and entrepreneurs, we too are human. And sometimes we have our own deep bruises. The bad actors online will try to find yours and press on them as a way to manipulate, control and hurt you.

If something is a deep bruise for you, you can create a wide circle around it. You can delete, block, evict, and scrub your own platforms of comments that try to press on your deep bruises. You can be clear on your own rules for what is allowed on your platforms and how people can engage.

I have a friend who has an old bruise around a family issue. After reading a comment on her website that pressed hard on that old wound, she spent the whole next day in bed; sad, fuming, and full of shame. Her plan? Her assistant reads all comments before approving them and deletes any that are triggering.

Many content creators have their assistants block and delete content that will trigger them before they have a chance to see it. You can be clear to your audience about what types of comments get deleted and what will get people blocked.

Farmer's Market Fist Fights

Imagine a farmer's market fist fight.

It's a pleasant sunny day at the farmers market, with people happily milling about. Until something happens. One person's apple cart gets tipped over. Then other apple carts are tipped.

Other people get pulled into the fight. If a CEO of the Internet or dumbass is standing around, they are always up for jumping in.

You can see the apple cart situation play out on Twitter in a flurry of retweets, threads and comments. It becomes a rabbit hole of chaos and thrown punches. On Facebook you can see it in comments where threads break off with dozens or hundreds of comments. It's the farmers market fist fight.

The more balanced people observing try to help clean up the situation or take a few steps back. It's not just the bad actors fighting you. The audience is fighting each other. Some people are for you and some against you, but in reality, you've lost control and it's barely about your work anymore.

Occasionally a large percentage of your audience gets triggered.

This is what happened with that article of mine on the curation site. The inflammatory and judgmental title that the editor assigned to this piece triggered a large percentage of the people who read it and they headed straight to the comments section to join the fight. The few people who actually read the article were trying to defend it. It was a mess.

I spent a fair amount of time in bars as a teenager. Honky tonk, loud, rowdy bars filled with middle-aged men who drank like it's their part-time job. I'm not sure if it was a very appropriate place for a teenage girl, but it was educational.

Witnessing a few bar fights, there are two ways bartenders can manage a group fight. In this farmers' market brawl, you'll need these bartenders' tips, because just like a bartender, you're in charge of this mess.

The easiest way to shut down a bar fight is to turn on the lights and turn off the music, declaring to all that the party is over. Online that looks like shutting down comments or temporarily archiving a Facebook group. I've seen influencers take a long break from social media to regroup, anywhere from a few days to over a month.

The worst brawls happened in Facebook groups in a flurry of new posts, tagging, and threads with 100+ comments. In extreme cases, I've seen group owners shut down the Facebook group for a few days to let people cool off and allow the moderators to rest and regroup.

The second option in a bar fight is to throw out the worst offenders. Find the troublemakers and kick them into the street. If there are a few people causing 80% of the ruckus, you could block them. Often the drama will die down without the loudest voices.

Either way, the most important rule of bar fights is: the bartender can't start throwing punches themselves (and you're the bartender). If the bartender starts throwing punches, all of the sane people sneak out the back because nothing good is going to happen after this. No matter how tempting it might be, don't start throwing punches.

In Chapter 17, we'll talk about how to handle it when the Internet turns against you either because you messed up or they think you messed up.

Apple cart moments are created from individual hurts and collective trauma, pain or shame.

Create a wide circle around your old bruises, to keep you productive and working. And when the farmers market fist fight breaks out, know that it's a reaction to something much deeper, older and persistent than you or your work at the moment.

SUMMARY

- A trigger is when an old hurt or shame, similar to an old bruise, gets pressed by the work you create.
- Add a *"Trigger Warning"* to sensitive content to give your audience time to choose for themselves if they want to engage with that past pain.
- The bad actors online will try to find your old bruises and press on them as a way to manipulate, control and hurt you. You can have other people scrub your platforms for you.
- Farmers market fist fights generally break out because of collective trauma, pain or shame. It's your job to manage the crowd, not join in the fight.

The Toddler Skillset

*"Criticism is something we can avoid easily by saying
nothing, doing nothing, and being nothing."*
—Attributed to Aristotle

I sat across from my therapist in a room perfectly equipped to be a conference room, with a long table that had sixteen chairs around it and a large TV monitor on the wall. He was pointing to a poster of emoji faces. It seemed like the kind of poster you would expect in an eight-year old's room. I imagine it was designed for kids, but here I was, in a month-long outpatient therapy program, staring at emojis.

Every time the question looped back to *"How does that make you feel?"* the therapist would lift up the emoji poster, with each emoji vividly displaying an emotion and said emotion neatly labeled underneath. He'd wave his hand across like it was the Wheel of Fortune wall.

All of this would be very insulting to me if I knew the answer to the question. But I didn't. I had a pile of emotions swirling around many of the life events that led me to this outpatient program, and I struggled to label any of them.

Since then, a big part of my adult journey has been to learn to *"feel my feelings."* To acknowledge emotions, label them, feel them, and move through them. Most therapists would say that this is an integral part of emotional health.

Bad actors aren't feeling their feelings. They are sharpening them into a blade and then turning them on you as a weapon. Instead of sitting with their own emotional experience, which is rather hard and challenging work, they are projecting their feelings on you in an attempt to hurt you enough that perhaps you will give in and change your behavior.

Maybe they can get you to stop doing whatever is causing this unpleasant emotion, so they don't have to deal with that emotion. Instead of working through their own frustration, disappointment or anger, they would rather you change your work, your brand, or your offer so they never have to feel their feelings.

Whenever an argument or request lacks logic, emotions get weaponized.

The common thread between the CEO of the Internet, Dumbasses, Trolls, and Apple cart people and what makes them all bad actors instead of thoughtful critics is that their ranting, bullying, and outrage doesn't really make sense. The reaction is disproportionate to the perceived offence.

If their concern was clear and valid, they wouldn't need to turn emotions into weapons. Instead, they could state their case logically, ask thoughtful questions, raise concerns, give constructive feedback, or make accurate observations. But logic generally isn't on their side. So the only thing these bad actors are left with to use against you are the emotional weapons of anger, shame, condescending, fear, mocking, bullying, outrage, and contempt.

Despite the huffing and puffing to make themselves seem strong and powerful, these bad actors are actually the most fragile among us. Unable to cope with the slightest discomfort. They would prefer a world made of pillows, so they never have to feel a feeling.

But your work isn't fluff, is it?

You created something engaging, thought-provoking, exciting, impactful, and honest. Your work isn't standing idly by; it's out there doing its damn job. If bad actors can't handle it, they should leave. Because you're not quitting.

Toddlers Skillset

For the last thirteen years straight, I've been raising kids under five years old. For a few years, my husband and I were outnumbered by toddlers in a 3:2 ratio. My conversations, travel, and free time has been very toddler-centric for a very long time.

I don't think of bad actors as evil people, necessarily; they are simply using the skill set that toddlers use.

When it's time to leave the park, toddlers don't take a deep breath to feel and acknowledge their disappointment. Instead, they resort to stomping, glaring, growling, yelling, and if that doesn't sway me, lying on the ground and screaming. All in the hopes that I will change my mind, and we can stay longer to play. That way they don't have to deal with their own disappointment about missing the park. This little person isn't *"feeling their feelings"*; they're using them against me to try to manipulate the situation because they can't cope with their own disappointment.

Having healthy emotional boundaries means I'm not going to join a toddler on the ground, kicking and screaming. I don't have to feel the exact same emotion they are feeling. I let out a sigh and say, *"I'm sorry that you are feeling disappointed and angry; but your five minutes are up and it's time to go."*

Eventually, with boundaries, toddlers outgrow these rudimentary tools of weaponized emotions because those tactics never work for them. After dozens of ineffective tantrums, toddlers are forced to learn new, more positive forms of communication and negotiation.

I suspect that the bad actors never learned new tools. Humans are designed for efficiency. We will use whatever tool works the best, with the least amount of effort. Bad actors never learned new tools because they didn't need to. They could rage, outburst, tantrum, and manipulate, and it was highly effective at getting what they wanted. There was simply no reason to change.

When someone is raging online: angry, and huffing about, I think about them like an overgrown toddler. Never having learned emotional intelligence, they now have to thrown themselves on the floor of the candy aisle at the store, kicking and screaming.

You don't have to react—you can leave them right there in their own emotions.

I know, better than most, how challenging it can be to develop emotional maturity and intelligence as an adult. So, I have a lot of compassion for the amount of hard work ahead of them. But unless you're a therapist and own an emoji poster, this isn't your job. It's not your work, your responsibility, or your problem.

When you see people turning their emotions into weapons to use against you, understand it's because their argument can't be rationally discussed or they are still working with a toddler skill set. Release yourself from either problem. Delete, block, or evict them. As my faith-based creator friends say, as a spin on *"catch and release"* we can *"bless and release."*

Leaving as a Form of Control

As a last (possibly desperate) act of control, the bad actor will get up off the floor, dust themselves off, and announce that they are leaving. One last little jab to try to pull you into the fight, manipulate you, or control you.

If I had a magic button that wiped all memory of me from the consciousness of every bad actor, I would push that button every single day.

The next best option is having the person realize that this relationship isn't going to work and them choosing to leave. To which, I'm thrilled they did a bit of the work for me.

The third best option is you or your team constantly blocking, deleting, and removing people. It's time and energy-consuming, annoying and expensive.

So, be eternally grateful when they show themselves the door.

A World Run by Bad Actors

In one last attempt to lend you some courage and confidence against these bad actors, I want you to imagine a world where all the bad actors get their way. If all creators go along with the bad actors' whims, all art stops. There are no more songs, writing, movies, social change. No one shares an original thought on social media. There are no more athletes (who are given a rather enthusiastic lot of bad actors.) There are no TV shows, or comedians, or news anchors. The brilliant architects, jewelry designers, and gardeners need to quit as well. Chefs, authors, and car designers just stop making new things.

At some point, every single creator has been told to stop by a bad actor. They've been told they aren't good enough, or what they make is rubbish. If bad actors get their way, creating grinds to a halt. All the art that makes life colorful, interesting, entertaining, and exciting goes away along with it. All new small businesses and entrepreneurship that move our communities and world forward cease at the whim of these bad actors. All for what? Because some strangers on the Internet can't handle feeling their own feelings or the process of communicating thoughtful ideas?

Hold back that tide. Creating and sharing is too important. The bad actor isn't worth the cost of the compromise.

SUMMARY

- Bad actors aren't feeling their feelings. They are sharpening them into a blade and then turning them on you as a weapon.
- As a last act of control, the bad actor will announce that they are leaving. Blocking, deleting, and removing people is time consuming, annoying and expensive. So be eternally grateful when they show themselves out the door.
- At some point, every single creator has been told to stop by a bad actor who thought their work wasn't good enough.

You Make a Thing;
You Make the Rules

"Givers need to set limits because takers never do."
—Rachel Wolchin

Back in my 9-5 job days, I had to attend Saturday morning meetings. I would get up extra early on Saturday because the meeting started an hour before the normal work day. Instead of making my kids blueberry and chocolate chip pancakes, which had been our routine, off to work I would go.

I dislike unnecessary meetings as much as the next person, but this one was extra special. This hour-long team meeting almost always devolved into the coworkers criticizing how each other dressed. It was a flurry of jabs like *"unprofessional, sloppy, frumpy, boring, punk and whorish."* As it went on, more people got pulled into the insults.

The only thing that made this Saturday morning treat even more unlikeable was that it was unpaid and mandatory without so much as a free donut.

I would try to nicely suggest to my boss that as owner and manager, he could simply create a dress code. He would huff and puff that he shouldn't have to because we are all grown-ups who should be able to figure it out ourselves. Instead of creating a few basic dress code rules and being clear about expectations, employees endured years of constant criticism and random insults from coworkers.

The owner didn't feel like he should have to create rules. We were all grown-ups, right? Everyone should do the *"reasonable"* or *"right"* thing, without ever being told what that looks like.

Maybe you sympathize that adults should be able to act like adults. You wish everyone had the same sensibilities, respect, and manners as you do, while never having to clearly explain what those would be.

Some people will naturally have your exact personal standards and conduct, but without creating rules and expectations and clearly communicating them, at some point, things will reduce to the lowest common denominator.

Please spare yourself, your fans, customers or employees this particular type of torture and own the fact that: **You make a thing; you make the rules.**

The internet is still rough and uncharted territory. There is no universal rule book to guide behavior. All that adds up to the fact that you have to make a lot more rules and be diligent on their clarity.

There are four categories of rules you'll need to make and communicate to your team, audience, customers or work partners.

1. Rules for yourself, to keep you working, productive and healthy.
2. Rules for your online presence and audience.
3. Rules for your brand, company, and products.
4. Understanding the rules of your industry or niche.

Rules for Yourself

One of my favorite authors, Seth Godin, says he never reads his book reviews on Amazon. His reasoning? The book has already been written, and he never plans to write it again. So why would he take criticism on something that can't be fixed? He did the best he could with the editors and proofreaders he had at the time. He says reading the criticism would only hinder him from starting the next book. He writes for his fans, not the critics.

Your personal rules help create specific boundaries around your time, energy and attention. Create rules about how you respond to email, social media comments, or requests for your time (work or social).

If you are meeting fans and customers at an event, do you greet each fan, a certain number of fans or for a certain amount of time? Do you do interviews or accept media requests? If so, which ones do you accept or deny?

Your personal rules also can help give clarity about how you show up professionally. One of my personal rules is that before work events, I always get eight hours of sleep. This helps me say no to late night gatherings or early morning meetings. I want to show up fully rested, present and in a good mood. Sleep is critical for that to happen. I also make sure I have some down time and alone time. As an introvert, too much *"extroverting"* can make me groggy and cranky.

As a creative or entrepreneur, very few people will make helpful rules for you. You have to know what works for you and advocate or hold those boundaries for yourself.

You don't need to publicly disclose all of your personal rules. They are created by you, for you. There are no set guidelines you need to follow. And you are welcome to change them as your brand and business evolves. But knowing them for yourself creates boundaries to help you personally thrive and frees you up to do your best work.

When I started my podcast, I mustered up the courage and emailed one of my favorite authors to see if he would consider being a guest on my podcast. He has a simple rule that helps him filter requests, *"after you get through 200 episodes give me a shout and if I can, I'll join you."*

He might field ten requests a day for his time. Imagine the amount of time and energy it would take to carefully consider each request without any parameters of what leads him to a yes, and what leads him to a no? The rules you write for yourself will help prevent *"decision fatigue."*

In a life of creating and sharing, you'll have to make a lot of hard calls, and carefully weigh a lot of decisions—both big and small. The rules you create for yourself will serve as shortcuts for the choices that get repeated.

Over the years, with trial and error (mostly error), I've come up with a few rules that work for me.

Here are a few of mine:

- All spam emails get marked as spam.
- I have 30 minutes a day to reply to emails and comments from fans. (I try to respond to every email. But some days I was spending 2-3 hours emailing and 0 hours creating.)
- I don't fight online. If you don't like what I'm creating, you are free to go, but I'm not going to fight. (I'm not perfect at this one. But I'm usually quick to see I've been pulled into a fight and try to bow out.)

A friend of mine attended a Taylor Swift concert very early in her career. She stayed after the show to talk to every single person and thank them for attending. That was probably a personal rule, and now with show audiences of over 50,000 people, the rule has shifted and transformed. But you can see how she still creates special moments with individual fans by attending proms, singing at weddings, and sending personal gifts. She has mastered staying true to herself and her brand while shifting the rules to accommodate her audience growth.

Sometimes I'll experiment with rules. Like, no new Facebook groups. Or only following people on social media I've met in real life. As your brand, your work or your business changes, you'll have to adapt the rules to fit.

No matter what you do, someone won't like the rule. Therefore, the goal can't be to create rules that every single person will like—they don't have to. Create rules that are helpful for creating and sharing your best work. Create rules that work for you. Rules that make sense for your business. Create the rules you want and change them when you need to change them.

Rules for Your Online Platforms

Up until this point in my creative life, I've never run a free Facebook group mostly because you need some really clear rules and constant enforcement. Moderating those types of groups is a thankless job. But if you make an online group, you had better believe you will need to make the rules. Rules about who can join, what people can say or post, what gets deleted, which threads get shut down and why people get evicted from the group.

Your online presence might be the bulk of your company or it might be a small digital footprint that benefits your brand. Either way, your digital presence will need its own rules.

Just like a workplace, it's your job to create brand culture. There isn't a correct or incorrect culture—it just needs to be clear to you, your team and the audience. It's probably perfectly acceptable to comment with a few F-bombs on Gary Vaynerchuk's platforms but less so on Oprah's, for example.

There are two types of rules to consider when it comes to your online presence.

First, how do you and/or your team *engage online?*

Do you respond to every comment? Do you engage in criticism online? Do you engage in customer service issues online or take those conversations offline?

What is your brand allowed to talk about? No matter where you draw this line, someone will disagree and be upset. Someone will be mad that you choose to talk about XYZ and they will let you know. And someone else will be mad that you don't talk about XYZ. If you or your brand wants to talk about politics, religion, social issues, or anything controversial, you of course are allowed to. It's your brand or company. Just know a certain percentage of people will be mad. The best way to deal with it is with clarity. *"This is my company, I will talk about XYZ. If that really upsets you, you might as well leave now."*

In a way, not being able to please everyone is a blessing. Because you get to please yourself. What do you want to talk about as a brand or company?

I follow Dan Price, the CEO of Gravity Payments, on Twitter and he almost never talks about his company. Instead, he gives insightful commentary of the financial inequality in most corporations and the overcompensation of most CEOs. He probably has 1000x the following and engagement talking about something he cares about rather than just promoting his company. And his company gets much more exposure for it.

The second set of rules to create are *how is the audience allowed to behave?*

What kind of criticism of you or your brand is allowed and what is blocked? What kind of viewpoints are allowed? For example, will you delete things that are prejudiced, hateful or threatening to you or others? Are people in the comment section allowed to fight with each other? How is that handled?

A few of mine include:

- Any hateful or dehumanizing comments are deleted.
- I/my brand unfollows anyone who posts those types of things.
- Criticism of my kids is off limits.

As a recovering people-pleaser and conflict-avoider, it's much easier for me to have these kinds of rules. It's less personal because it never was personal to begin with. I'm not blocking you from a Facebook group because I don't like you—only because you are trying to sell penis enlarging herbs, and we have a no-solicitation rule.

Rules for your Brand, Product and Company

Sometimes we forget that we are running a company. Especially if it's only us behind a computer: creating, thinking, producing, connecting, helping and improving in our little space online.

The area people often struggle creating rules for is in professional relationships.

A few years ago, I partnered with another company. At first it seemed like a fun way to help out a friend. We worked on a small project together. The scope of the project kept creeping and creeping, bigger and bigger. I tried to create rules around what I (my company) could do and what I couldn't do. Frustrations grew as expectations became more and more misaligned. Eventually, we had to part ways as I realized that despite my best efforts to create specific rules and communicate those clearly, we weren't going to get on the same page.

Behind the scenes of your brand, you'll have friends, collaborators, partners, employers and employees. If you made the thing, you have to make the rules.

In online spaces there isn't an HR department, a shared industry handbook, or shared expectations that help clarify how your company interacts with those groups of people.

People will ask you to work way below your normal billing rate. People will try to move your timeline (always forward in time, never later!). They will ask for more than you can give. You'll think you have shared expectations—only to find frustrations mounting. The scope of agreements will creep. You won't get paid on time. People will ask for favors out of the context of a relationship or will ask you to work for free.

There is no one to defer those issues to. The buck stops with you. Or if you have another person on your team to handle it, you still have to create the rule of how your company responds in these situations.

If I join the thing someone else made, like going to speak at someone else's event, I make sure I understand the rules they have created for the event—the written rules but also the unwritten ones. Do they want me to stay for the entire event? Should I attend dinners and mixers? Is it OK for me to leave for a few hours or am I expected to stay on site? These things might not be clear in the contract but if expectations are missed, it can lead to frustration for both of us.

If you feel pulled a hundred different ways in your work, it might be that instead of writing clear rules for yourself, your online presence and your company, others decided these for you by default.

Everyone won't share the same manners, assumptions, expectations, and sensibilities you have. Writing the rules could be seen as a burden, but it's also really empowering. You get to create the work you want to have. The rules you write, just like the garden fence, help protect that thing you made and allow your work to thrive.

Niche and Industry Rules

People who excel in a field know other people who do the same thing. Authors know other authors. Bodybuilders know bodybuilders. Politicians know politicians. Musicians know musicians. If you do a thing long enough, you should know other people who do that thing. You'll never hear of a world class runner who says *"Maybe it's odd, but I've never met another runner."* Or a famous fashion designer who says, *"I've been at this for 20 years but I don't really know other designers."*

Some will become your closest friends, and others will remain as acquaintances. It's like working at a big company—you'll have varying levels of collaboration, communication and depth of relationships. With one big *"except."* Except you're not connected like a company with clear company rules. Instead, you're navigating professional relationships where most of the rules are unspoken and vary from person to person.

If you're new to creating in a niche, you need to learn the ropes and the social norms. Most fields have their own culture. My friend Dr. Kerry Ann Rockquemore describes it like a wolf pack. Wolves are great at socializing wolf pups. They teach them how to be wolves. Let the pack teach you how to belong to the pack.

I was attending a personal finance event and someone walked up to me, said his name, shook my hand, and said, *"I want your business, how do we get that started?"* I reflexively laughed out loud, which he didn't seem to appreciate. I thought to myself *"Buddy, that's not how this wolf pack works."* I don't know if he read it in a book or watched some cheesy seminar that taught him that this is how content creators interact with each other. But he was 100% wrong. If you don't know your group's rules—the rules of the pack—you'll burn more bridges than you build.

Find as many people who are doing the type of thing you want to do. Meet them online or at events and conferences. And ask them. If you are doing something you aren't sure is acceptable, ask. If nothing else, when someone is generous enough to explain to you how you broke an unspoken rule, listen and thank them.

Recently at an event, I was sitting at a table with other podcasters. As a guest on a lot of podcasts, I mentioned one of the ways new podcasters mess up with inviting guests. A new podcaster was sitting across from me and started typing. He looked up and said, *"I'm literally going to write this down, can you tell me all the mistakes new podcasters make when booking big names?"* I was happy to list out 10 things and he wrote them all down.

Adult wolves are happy to socialize and teach wolf pups the rules of the pack because it makes the whole pack life better.

If the overzealous salesman at the personal finance event would have responded to my surprised laughter with, *"I'm sorry, I don't understand. Did I do something wrong?"* instead of being defensive and walking off, I would have happily explained to him that's not the vibe of this event, and it's not how the people in this community—or pack—tend to roll. This event is for building relationships, learning, and connecting with others. Closing deals happens only after those things are established. He could have learned and changed course if he was really interested in being part of this pack. Instead, I've never seen him in person or online since.

During an online class I was teaching about boundaries, we just finished the concept of *"you make a thing, you make the rules"* and *"clear is kind"* (which I'll discuss in the next chapter), when a few students had a simultaneous epiphany. It wasn't that others were disrespecting them or their boundaries, the frustrations were happening because my students hadn't created the rules and then communicated those clearly.

If you feel burned out, tired, attacked, or generally run down by your work or your audience and customers, check to see if you have created and are following the rules that will allow you and your work to thrive. And double-check that you communicated those rules clearly.

SUMMARY

- Your personal rules help create specific boundaries around your time, energy and attention.
- You create rules about how you and your brand interact online; your voice, tone, topics discussed and how you interact with the audience. You also have to create rules about how the audience is allowed to behave online.
- You'll have to create rules about how your company engages with customers, other collaborators, clients, and companies.
- Each niche and industry has social norms. If you seek out relationships and are eager to learn, people are generally happy to teach you because it makes the whole niche better.

Clear is Kind

"It's simple but transformative: Clear is kind. Unclear is unkind."
—Brené Brown

In the summer of 2020, as the pandemic rolled on, the issue of racial injustice came front and center with months of protests. My friends of color, especially my Black content creator friends, mentioned the fatigue and grief that was so overwhelming. So, I took a few thousand dollars and created a pop-up scholarship for female content creators of color, where I gave away $150 for self-care to everyone who applied.

I emailed my newsletter subscribers about the scholarship so they could nominate their favorite writers, podcasters, social media influencers, or YouTubers. At the end of the email, my *"p.s."* was added, stating, *"If you have an issue with this scholarship and feel the need to reach out to me to complain, please unsubscribe."* I was clarifying that my subscribers didn't need to agree with me, but I was not willing to argue about how I wanted to love and support people. If they needed a fight, it was time to show themselves the door—off my email list.

Side note: *Racial injustice will create group apple cart moments quicker than most topics. To the uninformed, the reactions seem disproportionate. But it's a few hundred years of collective trauma plus the current events that are driving these reactions. So a big reaction is an appropriately-sized reaction. If you are responsible for online platforms where people interact, always be mindful of collective trauma. Stronger rules and extreme clarity are needed to respect and protect the traumatized.*

Clear is Kind. Unclear is Unkind.

I use this idea in all my relationships: with my husband, coworkers, kids, extended family and friends to clarify and maintain boundaries.

When it comes to creating and sharing your work with a large audience or online, clarity is needed now more than ever. Because, like we have talked about, we are all learning how to navigate this online world together. The rules you create around your work, either in comment sections, social media, groups, events, or your inbox are going to be unique to you. Clear is kind.

Others Can't Know for You

It's hard enough to know our own boundaries. You are creating your own rules around how people can talk to you, or each other on your platform. You have expectations of your fans, clients, and partners that will be unique to you. Your personal rules might vary from the industry or niche rules.

I know some speakers who will engage with a heckler in the audience and others who will stop the talk or performance until that person is removed. Each creative or entrepreneur has unique rules, so you can't assume others will know yours if you haven't been clear about your rules.

Think about it like an autoresponder on your email when you're on vacation. If you generally respond to email in a day or two, people will be confused when two weeks go by with crickets. An autoresponder lets people know not to expect a response for the next two weeks and who to contact if something is urgent. The responsibility of clarity is on you to communicate. Others can't know for you.

A fan on Instagram direct messaged me to ask if I would follow his account. There is no way he can know the rules I have created for myself about who I follow and who I don't. I wasn't mad or insulted that he asked. Instead I could say, *"I only follow people I know in real life and authors I read."* Clear is kind because the other options are unkind. I could have not responded, been offended, or said, *"How dare you!"* Instead, I was clear about my rules. He responded, *"That makes sense, no worries."*

Almost every day, I receive pitches to be a guest on my podcast. Being clear about my guidelines is kindness. It would be unkind to mislead people or string them along when they aren't the right fit for my show. So I have created clear rules around who I have as a guest and communicate those.

Besides the trolls and dumbasses, who don't respect boundaries anyway, most boundaries are broken simply because we weren't clear in the first place. Ninety-eight percent of people will follow your rules, *if* you are clear about the rules.

Honesty Creates Trust

A few years ago, I organized a panel of speakers for an event. After the panel line-up was set, I was slated for a solo talk at the same time and couldn't moderate the panel anymore. All of these changes transpired months before the event, so the change wasn't on my mind by the time the event rolled around.

That was until friends of mine mentioned an issue with another panelist I had recruited. *"You really rubbed Brad the wrong way. He's pissed that you backed out of the panel. The only reason he said yes was because of you and then you bailed."*

Anxiety and pain gathered in my chest. Brad is the epitome of a nice guy and a dear friend. I had asked him to be part of the panel six months prior when I was to be the moderator. He had said yes, when in fact he really meant no. Or maybe he meant, *"I'll do it because we are friends, but I wouldn't do it otherwise."*

Unfortunately, the clarity wasn't there for either of us.

I felt horrible and awkward about the situation. And yet, how could I have known? How could I have fixed a problem I didn't know existed? Six months after the event, I had Brad on my podcast to chat about this idea of Clear is

Kind and how we can practice more clarity in our relationships as a way to foster trust.

Being honest and clear about your schedule, your desire, what you can do, what works for you in an agreement, or what you need creates trust.

I want people to also trust that when I say yes, I really mean it. I won't say yes, then secretly be resentful, bitter, or be critical of the person who asked. People often say yes when they mean no in order to be nice. But is that nice? I want people to trust that my *"yes"* is truly a *"yes"* and also to respect my *"no's"*. If I say yes, I mean it. If I say no, I really can't.

Often our *"yes"* has some conditions around it. Be clear about those boundaries. If I'm a guest on a podcast and have booked a 45 minute slot, I'll be clear up front that I only have 45 minutes or whether my schedule allows me to run a little long.

If you are vague or dishonest about what your *"yes"* looks like (in an attempt to be nice), the other person might unknowingly frustrate, disappoint, or damage the relationship with you. That creates the feeling of *"I never really know where I stand with them"* instead of trusting your yes and feeling secure in your relationship.

I'm clear about my boundaries, what my yes and no looks like, because I'm willing to protect my relationships—they are important enough to me to be *worth* protecting.

As Brad and I chatted on the podcast, we figured out there would have been a few answers that were more clear and would have protected our relationship. He could have said:

> *"I don't love committing so far in advance, but if you need someone last minute, I'd love to fill the role."*

> *"I will do it if you really need me, but only because I care about you. If you are able to find someone better, I'd rather bow out."*

> *"I'll do it because you're moderating the panel. Otherwise, I'd rather not commit to speaking on any panels, including this one."*

Find a Path Forward

A few years ago, I needed a freelancer for editing work with a 2-3 week lead time. The freelancer I was working with needed 2-3 months notice. After some honest conversation about what would work best for both of us, we could see that she wasn't the best fit for this specific type of work. It saved us months of frustration at my requesting things on a timeline that would be stressful to her or her needing more lead time that would delay my project.

When you are honest, it allows the other person to be honest as well. If I'm honest with my freelancers about when I need a project finished, it provides them with the opportunity to be honest about their lead time or work process.

Being clear about your rules or expectations opens up the conversation to find a productive path forward.

Like most content creators, I frequently get asked to work for free. Free labor is a big topic among content creators and especially women. Often our experience, expertise and knowledge are requested for free, not just from our audience, but from large companies. This is an area where you need clear rules, clearly communicated.

I have two simple rules. If it's something I have a current rate or offer for, I don't do that work for free. For friends, I might do something that I don't generally charge for, like an interview, writing a book blurb, or looking over their sales page. Also, when the *"pay"* is coming from *"exposure"* only you can know the true value of whatever exposure is promised. Never feel bad for saying no, because as the saying goes *"exposure doesn't pay the bills."*

For example, I have an established offer for my personal finance courses, coaching, speaking and brand sponsorship. So that's not something I offer for free. Being clear about that rule helps companies or potential clients understand how we can move forward with working together.

Clear is kind creates a path forward. With my freelancer, I knew to work with her for bigger projects that had a long lead time. I also knew I needed to find someone else for small quick turnaround editing work. If you have ever read my unedited writing, like my newsletter, you know why an editor is an essential team member for me!

I see too many people becoming frustrated and venting online that others don't know their boundaries. Instead of being clear about their own boundaries upfront, they express their outrage and disappointment when people cross these unknown, invisible lines. Being clear can open up more honest conversations and help you find a path forward.

30% of the Time

As part of our foster care training, my husband, Adam, and I took a series of parenting classes with a small group of excited and nervous soon-to-be foster parents. One of the classes was specialized for high need kids.

Part way through the training, you could feel the energy shift from nervous excitement to an overwhelmed apprehension. The parenting model they were teaching seemed impossible for any human to accomplish. Maybe the nanny robot from the Jetsons could pull this off, but not real humans juggling real family life.

The instructor saw the concern on our faces as the reality sunk in that none of us were cut out to be foster parents. In fact, I started to wonder who thought it was a good idea to send my biological kids home with me.

She asked *"This seems impossible to do perfectly, doesn't it?"*

We all gave a weary, *"Yeah, kinda."*

She continued, *"Well, the good news is that you don't have to do it perfectly. In fact, you can raise healthy, happy, and well-adjusted kids if you get this right 30% of the time. Do you think you could do this method 30% of the time?"*

The whole room perked up, 30% seemed very doable.

I'm not 100% perfect with Clear is Kind. I don't always clarify my relationship expectations up front (and with my personality type, I have many expectations!). I get annoyed with Internet strangers or fans who cross boundaries I haven't made clear. I get pulled into free work that then expands to be more than I ever would have signed up for until I'm resentful.

But it does get easier over time. Start with trying to be clear with your rules and expectations 30% of the time. You'll get more clarity on what those rules should be. And it'll get easier to communicate those to others.

The first, *"I don't do this type of work for free, but if you have a budget for this, I'm happy to figure out how we can work together"* type of email is hard to send, but after sending five or ten of these kinds of messages, it rolls off the fingertips. Remember—Clear is Kind.

Full Disclosure Not Needed

Applying the principle of Clear is Kind in our online relationships doesn't mean there has to be full disclosure of every detail and nuance for an honest conversation to happen. In any relationship, full disclosure is almost never needed. Instead, I look at what information, rules or expectations are true and helpful to open up a more honest conversation and create a path forward.

Once or twice a year I host retreats about personal finance, personal growth or entrepreneurship. Some people think the price to attend is a bargain while others find the pricing to be outrageous—and they proceed to tell me that. Being clear doesn't mean I need to start breaking out my spreadsheets, ranting about outrageous catering minimums and the cost of event space, or justifying making a modest profit. I also don't have to justify the cost by talking about all the past events I ran that have lost money.

A helpful and true response that opens up an honest conversation and creates a path forward might look like, *"This isn't the cheapest event out there. If it's out of your budget, I would suggest you consider events x, y, or z instead. Part of the expense comes from the venues I choose because I find them most conducive to the type of work we are doing. And partly because I pay my speakers, my professional ethics dictate that I never ask someone to work for free twice."*

When I share things with my audience that are particularly sensitive, challenging, or come out of my own pain, trauma, or mental health, I explicitly ask for no advice or suggestions. About 5-10% of the population somehow feels it's appropriate to give advice on anything that's shared online.

You don't have to provide full disclosure as to why unsolicited advice is inappropriate, unwelcome, or unhelpful. You don't need to explain why, when you are processing a challenging event, getting 1,000 opposing or critical opinions may trigger you or make the situation worse. It's perfectly acceptable to be clear that if they cross that boundary, they will be blocked, removed from a group or taken off your email list.

With "Clear is Kind" you will need to be making your rules clear over and over and over again, because new fans, new customers, new collaborators keep flowing into your life and work. The best way to keep those relationships healthy and productive is to have your new audience understand your rules by routinely being clear and up front about them.

SUMMARY

- It's your responsibility to communicate your rules. Others can't know for you.
- Being honest and clear creates trust in your relationships.
- Being clear can open up more honest conversations and help you find a path forward.
- You don't have to be perfect with being clear about your rules. Practice them 30% of the time.
- Full disclosure is rarely needed, instead look for what information, rules or expectations are true and helpful to open up a more honest conversation and create a path forward.

Emotional Boundaries

"A boundary shows me where I end and someone else begins,
leading me to a sense of ownership. Knowing what I am to
own and take responsibility for gives me freedom."
—Henry Cloud

One summer, I planted a sprawling garden across an enormous piece of land. As soon as the plants were in the ground, the garden got away from me. Weeds cropped up everywhere, rapidly outnumbering my plants ten times over. I would spend hours pulling the weeds only to watch an ocean of them return by the next morning. It was exhausting and frustrating. Like my garden, sometimes your creative life will also become overrun with weeds that will suck time and energy away from your work if you fail to establish emotional boundaries.

That's why you need boundaries for the work you are creating and sharing with the world. You need to give your work space, safe from critics and criticism, to flourish. Dealing with harsh feedback, trolls, and unhealthy people is like getting stuck in the weeds.

After the garden disaster, I've only ever planted in container garden boxes. The containers create a boundary for what is allowed into the garden space. These boundaries also help me focus on the plants inside to make sure they are being cared for with the right amount of water, light and nutrients. I'm responsible for what's inside my container.

In Montana, where the deer and the antelope play, our container gardens have an extra wall around the whole space. It's about a seven-foot tall fence with a gate, designed to keep out those high-jumpers. On the Internet, you might need to add a deer fence to your container garden. Deer are like the haters and bad actors, they don't want to just plant some hate, they will chew the whole thing down if you let them.

Think about emotional boundaries as having a dimension—a *thickness*. In marriage, that might be a tissue-paper thickness between your emotions and your spouse's emotions. Whatever they are feeling, you feel right with them. With your kids, maybe it's a bit thicker, as thick as a notebook. If your toddler throws a tantrum in the store, you might not get right down on the ground with them—kicking and screaming—but you feel the stress and anxiety rise in your chest.

As the relationships become more distant, the wall gets thicker. With your coworkers, maybe it's the thickness of a brick. Betty is in a sour mood, but you can generally ignore it and be fine.

What kind of space or thickness is healthy with us and the entirety of the Internet? I assure you it can't be tissue paper.

Glennon Doyle, author of *Untamed*, describes her boundaries as a moat around an island with a drawbridge. She has an *"only love in, only love out"* policy. Only love is allowed in. So that she can pour only love out. Anytime someone wants to try to plant hate, negativity, prejudice or harm on her platform, in her life or her family, they get blocked.

Some people will say, *"I don't care what anyone thinks."* But I'm not sure that's the solution. It's a simple solution, but caring about others is part of our humanity. Emotional boundaries need to be about *how much* you absorb others' emotions about your work while still being thick enough to keep you safe, healthy and productive. Emotional boundaries go both ways, they are also about how much you try to meddle or control your audience's emotions.

The Internet Stranger's Garden

So you have this nice little fenced container garden where you hang out, and your work flourishes in that defined, neatly-controlled space. Only you decide whose opinions are allowed in, who gets a voice and a say in how things are run in your space.

The reality is that every person in your audience gets their own little fenced-off space with some containers to grow whatever they want.

You are responsible for how people behave on your platforms or in your business. But you get *no* say in how they think or feel.

Emotional boundaries let the people in the audience, on social media, or in the comments section have their own thoughts and emotions, and keep those in their very own container garden.

People are allowed to:

- Think what they want to think.
- Assume what they want to assume.
- Draw the conclusions they want to draw.
- Believe what they want to believe.
- Leave if they want to leave.
- And feel how they want to feel.

And that's OK. They are free to plant whatever they want in their own garden space. But if they try to plant weeds on your platforms, in your garden space, they should be removed.

Market Watch sent a videographer to our home for a few days to create a short video interview about our journey from $55,000 of debt to becoming financially independent in our 30's. It highlighted the process we took and showed what life looks like now with raising five kids, camping and hiking.

When it was posted to YouTube, there were many nice and encouraging comments about what we had achieved and how we were prioritizing family.

There were also a number of comments about my bum. My apparently, very generous and ample, bum.

I just smiled and thought, *"I poured my experiences and knowledge into this work that was deeply personal, and this is what you want to take from it?*

An interest in how ample a fair skinned woman's behind can be? Okay. If that's what you wanted to take from the video, I'm glad you found what you needed from my work."

I try to give people the gift of letting them think and feel whatever they like. I'm not here to micromanage or control people's emotions or opinions in a crowd, in the reviews, comments or on social media. Of course, it's nicer when people like the thing I made—if it's a talk in front of a crowd, a class, an offer, or my writing. But whatever they think and feel, they are welcome to it. I'm not here to correct, adjust, or control my audience.

Emotional boundaries are neither cold nor calloused. It's a gift to let others be free to experience, think, and feel what they choose.

It's a waste of your energy and time trying to manipulate their ideas, interpretation, or experience with what you made so that it better fits your own intention.

Any explaining, defending, clarifying, and fighting I engage in is simply an attempt to control another's experience and manipulate it for my comfort, not theirs.

Marketing vs. Opinion

You can try to convince a group of people to try the thing you created. Maybe they will read the book, watch the movie, vote for you, or buy your service. You can do your best to help ensure they have a good experience. But at the end of the day, they will feel and think what they want to feel and think. And you get almost no say in that. It's not in your control.

Clever marketing might convince me to buy a book, but after I read it, even the most clever marketing can't convince me to actually like it. I either enjoyed it or I didn't. You can get the sports fan to watch the game, but when it's done, they will feel exactly how they want to feel.

After the customer or fan experiences the thing you create from start to finish, you have to allow that customer or fan to be free in their thoughts or feelings. Even if those thoughts are *"wrong"* in my view, or at least not what I had intended the response to be to my work.

It's like the gift of allowing yourself to be misunderstood. Set people free to feel outraged, bored, irritated, disappointed or however they like to feel. The bad actors will be so distraught feeling their own feelings that they will insist that you stop doing what you're doing—which you won't. And everyone else can feel and think and assume to their heart's content.

Give Yourself the Gift of being Misunderstood

One of the greatest gifts you can give yourself is the *freedom to be misunderstood.*

I firmly believe that people who *want* to understand will understand. There are also those dumbasses who will (likely intentionally) persist in misunderstanding you and your work. They love to spur on the fight. They take joy in watching you suffer under the weight of being *"misunderstood."* You aren't here for those people—and it's perfectly acceptable to let them know that.

In 2020, we saw the Ellen DeGeneres drama play out. She is known as the *"be kind"* person. Then a number of guests and employees came forward to say she's not, in fact, kind. Returning to the studio, she talked about the situation in her monologue for a few minutes. In short, she said something like: *I do believe in being kind. It's something I'm always growing in, just like other attributes. I'm not perfect. But I've done this show for 18 years, and I'm not a good enough actress to pretend to be something that I'm not for that long.*

Full stop.

I thought it was brilliant because she didn't engage in months of fighting, defending herself, battling against each story. She didn't respond to the CEO's of the Internet insisting that she be fired,or the dumbasses that only heard what they wanted to hear. She let the applecart people throw their fits, and she ignored the trolls with their mean one-sentence comments.

Those who want to hate her are free to continue to do so, but they didn't get to engage in a fight. Those who want to be fans and support her got a bit of clarification and a chance to move on and continue enjoying her work.

No doubt, I imagine it was an incredibly difficult situation for her to go through. If we were in her shoes, we might have wanted to defend against every accusation, providing lengthy explanations over and over. You might find yourself wanting, or worse, *needing* to feel understood by people who will never understand. There's a lot of downside in that approach.

Start giving yourself the gift of being misunderstood.

Because it also gives your true fans, customers, clients, and partners what they want: for you to get on with creating the work they love and that truly speaks to them—your true audience.

Even if the Internet is demanding an explanation, proof, answers, or personal information that are none of their business, you have no obligation to provide it. Don't waste your time and energy defending or proving yourself.

Just enjoy the gift of being misunderstood, and move on.

Dogs That Don't Fetch

Have you ever played fetch with a dog who doesn't fetch? Maybe it's a puppy who hasn't learned yet, but their owner is persistent and excited to teach them this trick. The owner keeps throwing the ball and the dog stares back with a *"Um, what's your point?"* kind of look. So the owner has to walk over and pick up the ball, and throws it again and again to the disinterested and confused dog.

The whole time the dog must be thinking, *"Are you having fun? I'm not sure what any of this has to do with me. Were you hoping for a reaction from me? Because buddy, this is all you. You can throw that ball, but you will need to go pick it up."*

As creatives and entrepreneurs, we need to be dogs that don't fetch.

Haters can throw criticism, insults and cruelty, but it's not our job to catch those things. The hater might as well go pick it up. Because we aren't going to pick up that hate for them. We play no role in that game. The haters can play if they want, but it has nothing to do with us. You'll watch the haters toss the insult, walk over to pick it up and throw it again. Hoping to pull you into the game.

The same thing can be said for taking offense to comments and actions. Whenever someone asks me, *"Aren't you offended by what that person said/did?"* I think to myself, *"I'm not picking that up. Just because someone threw something offensive doesn't mean I have to pay attention to it, catch it and hold on to it."*

The reality is that I have limited bandwidth to be offended, outraged or disgusted. I'm not going to waste it. Only I decide what to spend that *"offended energy"* on. I'm putting myself out there fighting against financial illiteracy and overwhelming consumerism to help a million people master their money, enabling them to create more meaningful and enjoyable lives. Some random person on the Internet isn't going to distract me from my self-defined mission just because they want to play fetch with an insult.

If haters want to throw that ball, they can go pick it up, but I won't. A thousand people might be trying to offend you and distract you from your true work at a time. You get to choose if and when you want to engage with that offense. Pick it up when you want to. But you're also free to let it lie.

Frustrations and Disappointments Aren't Fatal

People will ask you for lots of things: for a favor, a follow, an interview, something for free, a collaboration, sponsorship, or a hundred other things, and sometimes (often) your answer will be no. Sometimes, you'll lose that game or election that someone was hoping you would win. You'll support an issue that someone disagrees with. Your product won't be the right price for a particular customer, and they'll tell you about it.

Here's the reality: if you create and share enough work online, some people are *guaranteed* to be frustrated and disappointed with you.

Thankfully, being frustrated and disappointed isn't fatal. No one will die or be harmed by hearing *"no"* from you. You know your own boundaries and the rules you created, you know what time and energy you have to offer and the other commitments you have on your plate. Sometimes that means people won't get the exact outcome they were hoping for.

People—decent people—will feel frustrated or disappointed with you, and that's okay. Disappointment isn't fatal.

How do we know it's not fatal? Because we have all survived it. If you have lived in the creative or entrepreneurial space for a minute, you have likely experienced more than life's fair share of disappointment and frustration. And you survived.

I invite guests onto my podcasts—they say no. I ask to be on podcasts—they say no. I pitch ideas and am rarely given the gift of being told *"no"* in a direct, upfront way; more often, it's crickets that sing the song of no. Or worse, it's a *"maybe"*, which causes me to invest more time and effort that eventually results in a *"no"*.

Not to mention all the people who could buy your product or service and instead say no with their dollars. In my industry, if 4% of your fans purchase from you it means you have a great product or service with great marketing at a great price. 96% of people say *"no"*, and it's seen as a huge success.

In politics, if 40% of the voters pick the other candidate, it's a *"landslide victory."*

If 90% of the US population doesn't buy Beyonce's next album, it would be a triple-platinum smash hit.

In this work of creating and sharing your best work, you'll find yourself seeing and experiencing more disappointment and frustration than the average bear. Know that you'll be just fine. So will your fans, customers, collaborators, and partners. You can survive some disappointment and so can they.

Someone Will be Disappointed

If you say *yes* when you actually mean *no*, don't hold boundaries, don't follow your own rules, zig when you want to zag—ignoring your instincts, desire, and your plan, someone will still be disappointed and frustrated. Except now that someone is you.

And the other person has no idea why you are now out of sorts.

It might seem like kindness: frustrating and disappointing yourself so that the other person doesn't have to experience it. A lot of us were raised with the idea that if someone is going to be frustrated, disappointed, inconvenienced, irritated, or run ragged, that someone should be you. The philosophy seems to be: bend or break your boundaries, betray yourself if you must, just never let someone else feel frustrated or disappointed.

That's not kindness. Certainly it's not being kind to yourself, but it also isn't kind to the other person.

I've raised six children—four adopted, and two biological. Being a parent can be the most joyful work, but also the hardest.

I made a commitment to my children (and myself): *I'll never let my children ruin my life.* Thinking you have somehow ruined your parent's life feels like a cruel and heavy burden for a child to carry. For their sake, I'll never do that to them.

I made the same commitment when it comes to my work.

I don't think it's a gift to carry frustration and disappointment that could ruin your work in order to avoid being honest. If I ruin my life or my work, I want that to be entirely my fault.

You're Not a "9-5 Enabler"

It's never fun to have others frustrated or disappointed with you. But it's also not your 9-5 job to enable other people.

We all live in a world with boundaries, expectations, and rules. Every grown-up has to learn how to manage their own emotions, including frustrations and disappointments.

It's not your job to create this artificial, make-believe land with no rules and no boundaries, where every request is met with a yes—just so the person never has to experience any frustration or disappointment.

You aren't an enabler; you're a creator. Focus on your job—the work of *creating*.

SUMMARY

- You are responsible for what actions and comments are allowed into your container garden.
- Your audience can feel and think however they like about you and your work.
- You can convince someone to try your work, but you can't force them to like it.
- Save your time and energy for creating by giving yourself the gift of being misunderstood.
- Just because someone throws offensive or insulting words toward you doesn't mean you have to pick it up. You get to choose when to be offended.
- It's okay if people feel frustrated or disappointed, it's not deadly.
- If you try to protect everyone else from feeling frustrated, you will be the one who is disappointed, and your work will suffer as a result. It's not your job to enable other people.

Allow Your Work to Work

"Publishing a book is like stuffing a note into a bottle and hurling it into the sea. Some bottles drown, some come safe to land, where the notes are read and then possibly cherished, or else misinterpreted, or else understood all too well by those who hate the message. You never know who your readers might be."
—Margaret Atwood

In the middle of the night while I was sound asleep, I received an email from a mom in Scotland who was drinking her morning coffee and crying. An article I wrote about minimalism and motherhood had been published in a magazine in Australia and mailed across the world to her. She woke up early that day and read my work at the breakfast table. Tears of relief rolled down her face because the story I wrote about my own kids enabled her to make many of the same realizations about her own kids. She was a good mom. She was doing a good job. She was showing her kids the love they needed, and they were thriving.

While I was sleeping, this mom in Scotland was interacting with my work and my story—drawing benefit and comfort from it. My work was making an impact, even though I was never with her in person.

Your Work Lives Separately From You

My work, living separately from me, was going about its business, doing its job out in the world.

Your work might have been created in your mind and heart, but it lives separate and apart from you, as its own entity. Once you ship your work into the world, it has officially moved out of the house.

Because I write and teach people about personal finance and intentional living, most of my work is digital. All of it gets created in my head first. And sometimes it rattles around in my brain so much that it starts to feel like my work is *me*. It's my shadow and I never get a minute alone from it, so it's easy for it to become intertwined with my identity, if I allow it to.

So I send my work off on a work trip while I mentally and emotionally take a vacation.

Like Peter Pan who can send his shadow off to do its work completely separate from him, I send my work off to do its thing. I imagine chilling on the island while my shadow roams around the streets of London, making mischief.

Your work isn't your shadow. You're not sewn together. You can send your work off on its own work trip. You can take a staycation at home and just not be in the public eye for a few days. Turn off the Internet. Wear your jam jams. And imagine your work flying around in front of Big Ben or doing whatever your work does when you're not around.

Your Work Isn't You

Even though you made a thing that's filled with a lot of you—your story, idea, effort, and love—that thing still isn't you. You need to create emotional boundaries with the things you create.

Just like a picture of you will resemble you, it's not the whole you. It's not every emotion or every story and experience. It's an image—a snapshot. Just like a story about you isn't you. It's a story. A glimpse. A reflection of you who are at a brief, fleeting moment of time. You can create something that is personal and still not you. The work you create and share isn't an extension of yourself. It's the work. And you are you. There needs to be a boundary between those things.

No matter how personal your work feels or how much of your life you have put into it, your work isn't you. No matter how much you sacrificed to make this thing, it's not you. No matter how much inspiration you pull from your own taste, perspective, experience or personality, it's not you. Even if it is your own life story, it's the story of your life, a retelling, not your actual life.

Often the audience wants the creator to be the thing they create. They want the actor to be the character. The songwriter to be the song. Or the social media post to be the real life of the person. The athlete to be the game they played. The supermodel to be the pin up poster.

No matter how much your audience wishes and wills it to be true, you are not the thing you create. Don't fall into that trap.

Your work lives its own life, separately from you. Your words, offer or product is out there online, cruising the country or the world, doing it's thing. And you are right where you are, right now, reading this sentence. (A sentence I wrote months or years ago. I'm probably hiking right now or drinking a cup of tea.)

Your Work Isn't Your Child

I don't like the analogy that your work is your baby or your child, that you birthed it. I think it's a weird and generally unhelpful way to look at your work.

But sure, let's go with that analogy, at least for a moment.

If your work is a baby, when you send it out into the world, it's no longer a child; it's grown. A full-grown adult. You wouldn't send a baby to travel the world with a full-time job. If you are sending your work out into the world, it's because it's a fully-formed grown-up.

It can be your baby while you are tinkering with it behind the scenes, but once it's shipped, it's an adult.

If it's grown, allow it to do its work. Let it go live it's life out there. Don't follow it around, stalk it, or try to protect it at every turn.

There's no need to treat your work like a fragile toddler making sure that everyone is nice to it and treats it fairly. If it's a product, offer, social media post or piece of content, let it be grown—out in the world without its *"helicopter parent"* hovering protectively nearby.

Even with actual children, you know better than to follow them to job interviews and protect them from hard questions. It's not acceptable to tag along at their jobs and make sure all of their coworkers are treating them well. It's a weird thing to do for grown children and even weirder to do with your work.

Let your work do its job—without looking over its shoulder. You don't need to protect it or defend it on the Internet. You don't have to rush to its side every time someone says something mean or knocks it down. You can't (and shouldn't) micromanage your adult children's interactions—so don't micromanage your grown work.

Let your work do its job. If it was intended to be thought-provoking, let it provoke thoughts. If it should resonate on an emotional level, let it stir up emotions. If it was to help you find your customer, let it sift through and find the true fans instead of the people who will never buy from you.

Best Case, Worst Case

In this work of creating and sharing, there is a best-case and worst-case scenario.

Worst case: no one cares; no one sees it, hears it, or notices it. It's like throwing a rock into the soft snow. Your work makes no splash, no sound, it just disappears. Your work being ignored and unseen is the worst case scenario.

And the best case? The thing we actually want? It makes a ruckus. It generates a storm of attention. People buzz with praise and criticism. There is a hurricane of thoughts, feelings and comments. People write and talk at great length—both for it and against it.

Depending on your industry batting average, most of your work will likely be obscure. An actor might create 20 movies and only win one Oscar. The album has 12 songs and two are hits. A candle store created 97 fragrances before one gets mentioned in the media.

You might think *"Actually, Jillian, I was really just hoping for the praise part. Yes, it's great if it reaches a thousand, a million or a billion people, but can they all love it?"*

Even Harry Potter, the second most popular book in the world, still has some one-star reviews on Amazon. If you find a large enough audience, chances are that someone will still dislike the thing you create. The only way you can get 100% approval is to keep the audience size at about seven people, including your Mom and spouse. Although my husband can inadvertently make a face that is a dead ringer for a three-star Amazon review.

The way to find the people who enjoy your work is to wade through all the people it's not for. Finding your critics means that there was enough momentum behind what you created that even people who weren't your intended audience at least gave it a try. And that's a very good thing.

Science Experiments

I'm not sure I have any real scientific talent, but in high school I had a brilliant science teacher, Mrs. Generux, who made chemistry feel like an enchanted, magical, invisible world.

Molecules and elements unseen by the eye, created reactions and combined with other elements to form entirely new things. Despite the grueling math, I felt like I was peeking into a fairy garden to watch the magic unfold before me.

Like chemistry, your work will react and combine with others' lives and stories to form something entirely different than it was before. You can't control these reactions and compounds because you are only bringing half of the ingredients to the table. Your audience is as diverse as the periodic table. And they will bring all sorts of their own experiences, perspectives and stories to the *"chemical reaction"* with your work.

Every week I get letters about how my podcast has interacted with someone's life. The story I shared, or an idea I explained, combined with the moment in time of that person's life. All they have been experiencing, struggling with, or thinking about. Sometimes the reaction is exactly what I would have expected. Other times it's not at all what I could have predicted.

I can't predict or control what my audience brings to the table so I can't control what the reaction will create. But for that person, the work becomes something different, an almost mythical creature like Pegasus or Pan—half them, half your work.

In high school, a boyfriend sent me a mixtape with the song *Wildflowers* by Tom Petty on it. He said it reminded him of me. When I hear that song, it no longer has anything to do with Tom Petty, the band, the time it was written, or whoever it was inspired by.

Wildflowers is now my song. It's a song about my story. My joy and my struggle. It's about me being 17. It's about my mental health and how that shapes my relationships. It's about my fear of commitment and my desire for connection. Tom Petty's *Wildflower* song is no longer just his, it's now my song and my story. It has probably become something different than what Tom Petty planned or intended. I took what he made, and in some magical chemical reaction, mixed it with my own story until it was transformed into something new.

Not Your Work's Keeper

When you create and share your work, you don't exactly own it anymore. You might have copyright, a patent or inventory, but the work you sent into the world has interacted with the recipient and becomes something unique to them.

As long as you haven't done wrong and harmed others with your work, once it's shipped, you aren't the keeper of your work anymore. The work is free to do its work without you.

I'm sure someone owns the rights to the movie *"Dan in Real Life,"* but my copy of it has become something different than perhaps intended; it's the story of how my husband and I fell in love. It captures the hard-to-describe nature of finding someone and within a few days knowing you want to be with them every day...for the rest of your life. The movie perfectly reflects the feeling of our story, of finding your best friend and someone so compatible that fear and hesitation melt away. In the movie, it took Dan about three days to know he found the perfect woman. It took my husband two and a half weeks to buy a ring and propose to me, and I accepted his proposal with a heartfelt *"yes"*.

My work has done all sorts of funny and unexpected things out in the world—mostly wonderful and happy stories of how it mixed with others lives. But for some, it has renewed their passion for grammar and spelling. It has somehow inspired others to create a long list of unflattering words about myself and my life. Some people have taken offense, some people flattered me and some people probably thought nothing at all because it was so trite and banal.

At the end of the day, what your work does out in the world (except for potential harm) isn't much of your business at all.

I create my work with the best of intentions. I put all of my care, thought and love into it. I wish it the best as I send it out the door. I hope for good things from it. But with so many different chemical compounds out there, you are sure to have a few unexpected results. And a few reactions and outcomes that weren't intended.

I hope this book stirs up the courage and confidence for you to create and share your best work with the world. But perhaps, it just ignites your passion for English grammar. Because there are just too many damn sentences that start with a conjunction. And that's okay too.

SUMMARY

- You need emotional boundaries with your work once it has been sent into the world.
- Your work lives separately from you, it's out in the world, doing its job.
- Your work isn't an extension of you. It is, at best, only a glimpse.
- If your work were a child, it's grown, left home, and is out in the world.
- The only way for your work to find its intended audience is to wade through all the people it's not for.
- Like a science experiment, your work mixes with the stories of others and creates reactions you can't always predict.

PART 2

Overcome Imposter Syndrome and the Inner Critic

A fter you sort out how to deal with haters online and you have created the rules and emotional boundaries, often the very next critic you deal with is the voice in your own head.

Online criticism amplifies our inner critic, targeting our insecurity, old wounds, and doubts until they play on in a continuously repeating loop in our mind.

So you might get stuck in your head. That place where you question if you're good enough when so many people are better than you. You have great taste but are constantly disappointed with what you produce. You keep preparing but never creating and it becomes your favorite way to procrastinate.

It is in our minds that we wrestle with what our friends and family will think of us. What will they say if we fail, or even if we succeed beyond what anyone imagined?

In Part 2, we will tackle that inner critic head-on. So that you can show up, just as you are right now and serve the people who need your idea, story, product, or service. It doesn't matter that you aren't the most *"experty expert"*. None of us are.

Confidence and clarity come from doing, so you might as well get started doing the work you feel called to do.

The inner critic is a difficult foe, but when you win it over, it can be an even more powerful ally.

Imposter Syndrome

*"In any given moment we have two options: to step
forward into growth or to step back into safety."*
—Abraham Maslow

I n her best-selling book, *Becoming*, Michelle Obama spoke about impostor
syndrome. *"I still have a little impostor syndrome... It doesn't go away, that
feeling that you shouldn't take me that seriously. What do I know? I share that
with you because we all have doubts in our abilities, about our power and what
that power is."*

Jodie Foster said she worried winning an Oscar was *"a fluke"*. *"I thought
everybody would find out, and they'd take the Oscar back. They'd come to my
house, knocking on the door, 'Excuse me, we meant to give that to someone else.
That was going to Meryl Streep.'"*

Which is funny because Meryl Streep told Ken Burns during a 2002 interview for USA Weekend:

*"You think, 'Why would anyone want to see me again in a movie?
And I don't know how to act anyway, so why am I doing this?'"*

I haven't met a person yet who has never felt a twinge of imposter syndrome. The person who can say *"I've never done this kind of work, at this level, but I know I'll be amazing at it. Better than anyone else. Actually, even though I'm new to this, I deserve to be here more than they do."*

I'm sure the person exists, but to move into new areas, stretch yourself in new creative and entrepreneurial ways, and not have a twinge of imposter syndrome is another issue altogether: *unearned confidence.*

Imposter syndrome strikes at two points in our creative journey. First when we are starting something new, then again when we are growing into bigger or different places.

It boils down to this simple reality: if you're continuing to grow, challenging yourself, and trying new things, imposter syndrome will be there to meet you every step of the way.

When I first started coaching, I started at a very modest rate. But even charging that rate to my clients created serious anxiety and doubt in myself. The funny thing with imposter syndrome, it doesn't always attack us in a rational way. See, I was confident in my work and the transformation I could provide for clients.

The things that I got hung up on were my usual, old insecurities. I was from a small town in Montana. I didn't have a master's degree, or a doctorate from a fancy college, or any college for that matter. Because I had worked a lot of blue collar jobs or never earned a high salary before, I was now bothered that my coaching was earning more than other people I cared about who were working longer hours for a lower rate.

None of those things impacted the quality of my work. But those things triggered my imposter syndrome.

As I settled into my work, those old fears faded. I raised my prices two or three more times with little resistance, until I hit a certain dollar amount. Then, all those old insecurities flooded back to me again. It was still on things that were neither here nor there. My clients didn't care where I grew up or how much money my family made. Those things made no impact on my work.

Imposter syndrome ties us up in knots of doubt. The trick to untying the knot is knowing you're not alone and hopefully having conversations with people who understand.

Amateurs and Professionals

Seth Godin talks about the difference between amateurs and professionals. I would like to add one more distinction between them.

Amateurs don't feel imposter syndrome. Because if they aren't creating and shipping their work and growing in the process, they're a hobbyist. And hobbyists don't experience imposter syndrome.

In my free time (which is minimal with five kids at home, rental properties, and a business to manage), I practice hand lettering and watercolor painting. I'm not particularly good at either and yet I've never experienced imposter syndrome. It's because I'm a hobbyist. I'm not shipping this work into the world in a way that a professional would—I'm not invested in the outcomes, and I don't feel I have anything on the line.

It's in the vulnerability of making something we care about, turning *"pro"* and in the process saying we are that person who makes this thing and sharing it with the world that imposter syndrome is triggered.

In other fleeting, free moments I'm quietly writing a screenplay. Again, I've never felt imposter syndrome about this, because there is no scenario where I would ever share that with another soul. I'm writing it for me, simply because I enjoy spending time with these characters. I'm not claiming to be a screenwriter. I'm not sharing it with people hoping that it will be bought. I'm an amatuer, a hobbyist.

But I guarantee the minute someone asks to read it, the imposter syndrome would hit me like a wave that knocks down an unsuspecting child on the shoreline. I would trip all over myself explaining how I'm not really a screenwriter, how this is crap, that it was just a hobby, and that I have no idea what I'm doing.

It's not that the professional is more experienced, or more skilled. They are just willing to say, *"I am a screenwriter and I'd love for you to consider mine."* The professional ships their work and stands by that identity.

High School Basketball

In high school I had the great fortune of playing basketball for Coach Lackner. Our small, rural high school might have had 40 girls in a good year. When trying to create a winning team, he didn't exactly have a massive talent pool to pull from. Instead, what we lacked in ample raw talent, he compensated for with training.

Lots of training. He had a bit of fame or infamy for our physical training routine. The first two weeks were always rough. Despite our best intentions, no one showed up in great shape after a long and lazy summer.

The hardest training came at the end of practice when the team would line up at the end of the court to run lines. Soon we would all be doubled over, gasping for air. Someone would inevitably run off the court to vomit. And someone would break down in tears.

It was in the midst of all the vomit and tears that I learned one of the most valuable life lessons in the creative and entrepreneurial life:

Just because there is vomit and tears doesn't mean you're doing something wrong. In fact, you are probably doing exactly what you need to do to get where you want to go.

It is the same with imposter syndrome. Just because you feel imposter syndrome doesn't mean you're doing anything wrong. In fact, you are probably doing exactly what you need to do to get where you want to go.

Feeling imposter syndrome means you're trying and growing. It means you're creating work as a professional and shipping that work as a professional.

If you never experience imposter syndrome, we may have a bigger problem. You're playing the game too small or too safe. You're likely playing every game you as an amatuer.

Never read the feeling of imposter syndrome as a sign you're doing something wrong. It means you're doing something right.

I love this story from author Neil Gaiman.

> *"Some years ago, I was lucky enough to be invited to a gathering of great and good people: artists and scientists, writers and discoverers of things. And I felt that at any moment they would realise that I didn't qualify to be there, among these people who had really done things.*

On my second or third night there, I was standing at the back of the hall, while a musical entertainment happened, and I started talking to a very nice, polite, elderly gentleman about several things, including our shared first name. And then he pointed to the hall of people, and said words to the effect of, "I just look at all these people, and I think, what the heck am I doing here? They've made amazing things. I just went where I was sent."

And I said, "Yes. But you were the first man on the moon. I think that counts for something."

And I felt a bit better. Because if Neil Armstrong felt like an imposter, maybe everyone did. Maybe there weren't any grown-ups, only people who had worked hard and also got lucky and were slightly out of their depth, all of us doing the best job we could, which is all we can really hope for."

Neil is right. That's all we can really hope for. Work hard, get a bit lucky, stay in the discomfort of being slightly out of our depth and do the best job we can.

SUMMARY

- Imposter syndrome is evidence that you are learning and growing— exactly as you should.
- Amateurs don't experience imposter syndrome because they are acting like a hobbyist, not a professional.
- Imposter syndrome is something almost everyone feels at multiple points in their journey. Know you're not alone and also that you can find others who can relate.

Family and Friend's Opinions

*"Our greatest fear should not be of failure but of succeeding
at things in life that don't really matter."*
—Francis Chan

When I started writing about personal finance, one of my first mentors was Ryan Nicodemus of The Minimalists. My concerns about what friends and family might say were a recurring topic of our chats. Personal finance can be a taboo subject to be so open about, especially among our own inner circle.

When I interviewed him for this book, he asked after all my fear and concern, *"How did it go with friends and family?"*

I responded, *"Turns out my family and friends aren't anywhere near as interested in my life and work as I imagined they would be."*

Concerns over what your friends and family might say when you start, if you succeed or fail, might seem to belong in Part 1 about the outside critic. But I wanted to add it to the inner critic because while I've had a dozen slightly uncomfortable conversations with family or friends about my work, my success, and my failures, I've had a thousand of those conversations in my head. A thousand is probably a modest estimate.

The fear centers around disapproval or disappointment, and both are tough to receive. It strikes the creative and entrepreneur at three main points.

- When you are getting started with something new
- When you fail
- When you succeed

Incredibly supportive and unsupportive families both present challenges. So in this chapter, we will tackle all three points from both sides of the coin.

Getting Started

In the last chapter, we talked about how getting started triggers your imposter syndrome. Now you have your friends' and family's reactions which might compound that.

My husband and I saved for ten years to buy our first home. We had saved enough to buy a reasonably nice house. Instead we opted to buy the ugliest home we found so we could have enough left over to buy our first rental. The plan was to fix it up ourselves, despite the fact we had almost no experience or tools. There were no Chip and Joanna Gaines to hold our trembling hands and tell us everything would be OK. Drew and Jonathan Scott of the *"Property Brothers"* were not there to assure us they would take care of everything. It was just us, with no experience and shaky confidence at best.

We bought this ugly house after a single 30-minute visit and no home inspection. The house had obvious and extensive flood damage in the basement along with mold. We gave the sellers a pile of cash and got the title a few weeks later.

Walking my family through for the first time, I knew this house took a strong imagination. My family was quiet and looked a little scared. My grandmother, in a low soft voice, said, *"Oh, honey, you're not going to live here, are you? With my grandson?"*

I had a vision for the home. Just like creatives and entrepreneurs have a vision for their work. And not everyone has the strong imagination or vision that you have.

My grandma's concern was valid. The basement was covered in black mold. Sometimes those closest to us want to protect us from risk, fear, uncertainty, and failure. But that's because they aren't sure *they* could withstand those things. It doesn't mean *you* can't.

The other side of the coin is unearned confidence from those you love. A number of years back, a close friend was up for a very prestigious award. A group of friends and family were gathered around, piling on the encouragement. *"You'll be amazing! Of course you'll get it. You always win, this won't be any different. I know it will happen!"*

I could see him getting uneasy and shifting in his chair. He slowly said, *"I appreciate the vote of confidence. But this is actually an incredibly exclusive award. The odds of me winning are statistically tiny. Just understand that the most likely outcome is that I won't win."*

Unearned confidence can add to the pressure and fear of failure and makes getting started on your work that much harder. It activates that inner critic *"What if I do this and then everyone knows I'm not as good as they think I am?"* Disappointing those we love is a heavy burden to carry.

If either of these influences would stop you before you even start: don't tell people. Not everyone needs to know, or know the full scale of what you are working on. I wrote anonymously for over two years because I was worried about the feedback. Anonymous street artist Banksy is doing just fine.

When You Fail

Creative and entrepreneurial life is a life of failure. A hundred little failures. A few big failures. And 95% of the rest of it probably could have gone a bit better. There is only a sprinkling of unencumbered, unqualified, sparkling successes by every single metric.

When you have unsupportive family and friends, out roll the standard lines, *"I told you this was a bad idea." "I don't know why you even started this." "Of course it failed, I knew it would. You never listen to me."* And more of the same.

But this almost always comes from those unfamiliar with the creative and entrepreneurial game. They don't understand the rules. The fact is that the only way to truly fail in the game is to take your ball and go home, never to return. You grow and learn the most in the projects that are a struggle for you. The struggle is what makes you a better player in the game.

Don't take to heart the advice from those totally unqualified to referee the game.

The other side of the coin: the supportive family. It's almost more crushing when you fail in front of them. The weight of their disappointment and embarrassment on your behalf is hard to shake off. All the love and support they have given feels like they wasted it on you.

But chances are they are also just as unqualified to referee this game of the creative and entrepreneurial life. Because they are so supportive, you might be able to explain how the game works: *that you learned and grew from this. That you're happy you tried. Next time will be better. It's a long game, and you're only starting out. You'll take everything you learned about yourself and your project and go into the next thing more equipped.* In short, when you fail in front of supportive friends and family, you might need to be the one cheering *them* up and buoying *their* spirits.

When You Succeed

Celebrating your success is in the wheelhouse of your supportive family and friends, but even for them there can be an awkwardness about how to acknowledge it. For them your success can feel like visiting a nudist beach. For those not familiar with such places, there is an uncomfortableness of where to look. Interactions around success can feel like that. Your friends and family aren't sure where to look at your success. Do you acknowledge the naked elephant in the room, or pretend it's not there?

In both failure and success, you're growing and changing. You're learning new things and meeting new people. As a result, even supportive friends and family can be triggered with fear of all these changes.

It's hard for your friends and family to say, *"You're growing and changing and I'm happy for your happiness. But I also feel scared, judged, and insecure by how different we are becoming. I feel like I don't know who you are becoming. And I'm worried about how all of this will change our relationship."* So instead they might criticize, seem distant, or avoid the topic all together.

Change is hard. Hard for you, but also hard for others who perhaps didn't opt into how you are changing. Sorting through these fears is their work to do—you can't force them to do this work. Instead, with my wonderfully supportive family members, I try to build a bridge of interests and topics. I make sure to still join them in their world, and continue to find ways to invite them into my new world.

The other side of the coin is the family that always struggles to be supportive, even when you win.

Watching you succeed can trigger deep emotions in other people. It will touch on their own shame or regret for not living up to their own potential. They might feel your success is unfair. Jealousy of what you have or what you accomplished can creep in. They might worry you are somehow judging them, their choices, work or lifestyle.

One of my daily affirmations is a quote from Oprah Winfrey. In her 20's as she grew in fame, wealth, and success, people from her past started saying things like, *"Well, aren't you full of yourself."*

Oprah had to start looking at her success differently. She didn't want their negativity to become a stumbling block. She adopted this more helpful perspective.

"Now, I work on being full. So full, I'm overflowing without pride or arrogance but with gratitude." She continues, quoting from Maya Angelou, *"When you see my passing, it ought to make you proud."*

When you try to change generational norms, there are often those who want to pull you back to things that feel familiar to them. Maybe familiar is similar types of work, similar amounts of income or debt, unproductive habits, and unhealthy relationships.

Your work isn't to shrink back to places that feel more familiar and comfortable for others. Your work is to become so full you can overflow for others. Without pride or arrogance but generosity. You're growing and changing to be able to do the work you're called to do. Your best work.

SUMMARY

- Your friends and family will struggle with you getting started, failing, and succeeding. The more you know how to navigate these situations, the more you can help them.
- Amazingly supportive friends and family struggle to support and encourage you just like unsupportive family and friends.
- When you're growing and changing as a person (and in your work), friends and family might feel scared, judged, unfamiliar or unsure how to articulate that fear.

Confidence and Clarity Come In Doing

"You don't have to see the whole staircase, just take the first step."
—Martin Luther King, Jr.

"Clarity comes from action, not thought."
—Marie Forleo

Girls' basketball captured the collective attention of my tiny Montana hometown. For me, it had all my attention, long before I ever laid hands on a basketball.

As a young girl watching the girls's high school basketball team, I dreamed and wondered if I could do it. *"Would I be fast enough, tall enough, skilled enough, and cool enough under pressure?"*

I could have asked a thousand people (which would have been every single human in our town plus a few horses). I could have read books and studied videos and taken classes. I could have wondered and visualized and read affirmations. All of those things have a time and place, but none of them would have given me the clarity and confidence that I could play basketball.

Confidence and clarity come in doing.

I had to play basketball. Over and over and over. In the process of doing, I knew what I could do and what I couldn't do.

Before people start creating and sharing their work, their minds swirl with questions.

"What if I'm not good enough?"

"What if I don't like it?"

"What if no one else likes it?"

"What if it fails?"

"What if there isn't a market and no one buys?"

I imagine people expect me, as a coach, to fill them with confidence and clarity. *"You'll be amazing! You'll love this. It's a perfect fit. Everyone else will love it too!"*

That's not how confidence and clarity work. An outside person can't give you a transfusion of clarity and confidence. You can't sit on your couch and muster it out of thin air. At best, you can borrow my confidence and clarity for a short while, just to get started, but your work and business can't run on this alone. You have to get those things for yourself: Clarity that you know the plan, or the process to make your work succeed, and the confidence that you will figure it out.

Confidence and clarity come from doing.

People ask me, *"Am I talented enough, smart enough, capable enough, or cut out for creating things and sharing? Will I enjoy it? Will it bring me joy? Will others want to buy it?"* Probably to their disappointment, I say, *"I don't know."* I might even think so, or believe so, but ultimately you can't really know until it's done.

So my most honest answer is, *"Let's try and see how it goes."*

Doing it is the only way you will figure it out.

If you don't feel like you have clarity or confidence that this thing you want to create will work, just start.

No amount of preparation will replace the simple act of beginning to play the game.

When I created my first event, I had about as much preparation a person could have without actually doing the thing. Part of my husband's work in the military was to help organize events for soldiers and their families, marriage retreats, family retreats, and personal growth and leadership events.

Having attended about twenty-five of those events, I had a good sense of what I wanted and what I thought would work. The perfect blend of smart speakers, a beautiful setting, moments of real connection, opportunities to explore and be in nature, and relaxing meals together.

But that still didn't change the fact that I had never done this. I didn't have perfect clarity on the event or perfect confidence. Instead, I had to settle for high hopes for the end result.

I treat every project, offer, service, and product as an experiment the first time. Because it is. And as an experiment, I plan to learn about how to improve what I have created, adjust course, and make it better next time.

It's through doing that I earned the clarity of how to craft an amazing event. It's through doing that I have the confidence that what I put together will work. Not that I stop viewing it as an experiment. Since I'm a "better-er" by nature, one of my greatest joys is making things better. In that process of constant improvement, my own confidence and clarity grow.

SUMMARY

- Confidence and clarity are earned through doing.
- You can borrow others' confidence and clarity, but it's only a short term solution.

Ch 13

Taste vs. Skill

"All of us who do creative work, we get into it because we have good taste. But there is this gap. For the first couple years you make stuff, it's just not that good. It's trying to be good, it has potential, but it's not.... It is only by going through a volume of work that you will close that gap, and your work will be as good as your ambitions."
—Ira Glass

Months of planning went into my podcast, *Everyday Courage*, before we even started recording. A whole group of creative, smart, and experienced people had helped my show get this far. I went into the podcast recording week full of excitement, studied, and prepared. It was a grueling schedule of recording 22 episodes, but I left with that deep satisfaction that comes from preparation and hard work.

Driving to catch my plane, I put on a podcast episode with two of my favorite creatives, Rob Bell and Elizabeth Gilbert. Their conversation was sparkling, energizing, funny, smart, and incredibly brilliant.

Panic, shame, and regret instantly welled up in me. Listening to that episode, I realized that all the work I just finished was shit in comparison.

And that's not the worst part. What nearly crushed me was knowing those 22 episodes were the best I had in me. And the only way to get better was to *keep going*. I had to continue to produce disappointing, stilted, and mediocre work, and muster all of my courage to share that work with the world.

In an interview recorded that week, I had talked about the very quote by Ira Glass you see above. Now, with hot tears rolling down my very weary face, I let its impact on me sink in.

Ira Glass is right. You got into your craft because you have incredible taste.

She has an eye for typeface design. He can pull together an outfit. She appreciates comedy and timing. He has a taste and eye for coffee and the passion for customer experience. She hears a stirring sermon and wants to be the one to create that passion and share it with the world.

But your skill doesn't match your taste. Yet.

It's a grind. Everyday. Showing up. Pouring out your creativity, intuition, knowledge, and skill, only to create something that is, at best, mediocre and even that might be generous. Instead of deep satisfaction, your heart sinks into frustration, disappointment or worse, shame.

My only saving grace in that moment was the fact I had been here before, creating something I wanted to be amazing, only to watch it fall flat.

I've prepared sermons that I hoped would spark a life-changing event: they didn't.

I've written blog posts I thought were clever: they weren't.

I've given interviews I intended to be clear and insightful: didn't happen.

I started a business I wanted to be successful: failed horribly.

I've made art, written poetry, given speeches, and have now written a book—this one. The first one is never the best.

That's not how skill-building works. It's a slow and steady process. Each attempt is like a thin stone dry-stacked on the last attempt. Each one falling short of the top of the wall. But with each one, you climb an inch taller. Dry-stacking rock walls is patient work. Each stone needs to be set with care and thought. The only way to help your work match your taste is to keep stacking, one attempt after another, stone after stone.

One of my kids has an incredible eye for art. As a very young child, her use of color and shape surprised adults. But she has one fatal flaw to becoming a great artist. She gets incredibly frustrated and short-tempered when her skill doesn't match her taste. Instead of using that frustration as fuel to keep trying, the discomfort causes her to quit.

She's an incredibly bright child and most things in life come very easy for her compared to her siblings. She has an underdeveloped *"struggle muscle."* As soon as things are a struggle, she quits.

Feeling your feelings means you need to feel and move through the disappointment, shame, frustration, and embarrassment. The most successful people I know can navigate through that hard place.

It's like being caught in a blizzard. The only rule is: never stop walking. If you stop and lay down to rest, you might freeze to death. Keep walking, embrace the difficult moments, and grow your *"struggle muscle."* The only way to make it to the other side is to keep walking through the storm.

SUMMARY

- You got into this industry because you have incredible taste.
- The only way your taste can match your skill is through repeatedly creating work that disappoints you.
- Lean into that discomfort as the price of improvement.

Myth of the "Experty Expert"

"Who's to say who's an expert?"
—Paul Newman

When I was seventeen, I followed my Dad's footsteps and joined the Army National Guard. I hadn't been to basic training yet, so I borrowed my dad's uniform and boots. I tore off all his earned patches, leaving only the *"Johnsrud"*, and donned that gear as I spent one weekend a month for a year with mostly middle-aged veterans of Desert Storm.

Each drill weekend, a few of the soldiers would lead hour-long training sessions. The surprise among the group was evident when I raised my hand to lead a training about maintenance and care of the M16 rifle, but I was given permission to deliver this session for the following month.

I spent all month studying the handbook and memorizing everything I could.

The next month at drill, I checked out an M16 and stood in front of the class. Before me were combat-tested war veterans, deeply familiar with this weapon. I wore my dad's slightly oversized uniform and gave a tutorial on a weapon that I had never even held before that morning.

No one, including me, had any doubt I was the very least qualified person to teach this class.

You might ask yourself, *"Who am I to (write, teach, coach, speak, offer this product or service)? There are so many people better than me, smarter, more skilled, experienced, talented, educated, or accomplished."*

And I'd say: *"Ok. Sure. And?"*

You might argue, *"But there are BETTER people for this job."*

And I'd say: *"Ok. Sure. And?"*

They might be better. And we still need *you*. Your voice, your story, your perspective, your taste, your availability, your price, your skill.

More Than One Is Needed

Meryl Streep is probably a better actor than you or me. Every role she plays amazes me. She helps me get lost in the story. Because she is better than us, should she play *every* role? In *every* movie? Forever? Would that make the movie industry better? Because you and I do agree that she's better than either of us.

It doesn't work like that, does it?

Even if your idol is better than you by every conceivable measure, we still need you. There can't be only one artist, singer, pastor, bakery, coach, clothing designer, or coffee shop.

You don't have to be the *absolute best* to show up, create your work, and share it. Your talk can be helpful. Your music, moving. Your social media feed, inspiring. Your videos, educational. Your stand-up, hilarious. Even if you aren't the most *"experty expert."*

Still Someone's Favorite

You don't even have to be the best to be someone's favorite. I'm not the best writer, podcaster, or coach. But I'm someone's favorite. Against all odds. There is some combination of my voice, my story, and my perspective that connects with a person.

People who subscribe to my email list will email me to say that in a sea of emails, mine is the one they always open and read, sorting through all the other email to find mine. My email newsletter isn't the best on the Internet, by any metric. But it's still someone's favorite.

You might not be the best, and yet you can be someone's favorite.

Not the Best, but the Best Option

You don't have to be the best in order to be someone's best option.

When my coaching clients are struggling with this, I'll turn the tables on them. They are feeling unsure if they are good enough to help others because they know their taste is better than their skill and there are more skilled, talented people out there.

I'll ask my clients *"Why did you decide to work with me? There are so many experts far more experienced and qualified than I am."*

Long pause. I'll let the awkwardness of this question hang for a moment.

"I'm not the best in my field by a huge margin. Brené Brown, Seth Godin, Donald Miller, Ann Lamott, Elizabeth Gilbert, Amy Porterfield, Michael Hyatt, or hell, Oprah. They all are miles ahead of me. I'm merely walking in their footsteps. Why did you choose me over Oprah?!?"

Even longer pause.

Slowly the light bulb brightens. I'm not the best, but I'm still the best option. I'm not the best, but I might be their favorite. I'm not the best, yet my work is still incredibly helpful for them.

There might be more qualified, more skilled, more talented people out there than you.

AND you might still be the very best option. Your availability, your price, your perspective, your offer might be the best fit for what they need. Often the most skilled, talented, educated, and experienced person isn't always the best person for the job. People are needed at every skill level, every price point, every level of availability.

You don't have to be the most experty expert to be the right person for the gig. Mucha might be my favorite painter, but I'm glad that others paint too. I'm thankful for his work, just as I am also thankful for the designer who created my book cover.

Loosen the knot of comparison. Because in the life of creating and sharing it can hang you on either side. I hope someone reads this book and thinks, *"I could write this book better. I have a better story, perspective, and skill."* And I hope they do write a better book. I also hope to write a better book after this book. Cheer others on and cheer yourself on as well.

Hamilton might be my favorite soundtrack. And I hope someone writes an even better one. And I hope Lin-Manuel Miranda's next play blows us all away. *Because the world is wide enough for both Hamilton and you.*

There is enough space for what you create. The Internet has made the table longer still. Stay in the game long enough, and I can almost guarantee you will be someone's favorite.

Standing in front of those soldiers that day was one of my greatest life lessons in leadership, teamwork, and courage.

Imagine if that would have happened in a corporate setting. Someone who wasn't even qualified to work there, had no training or experience, and was the most junior person, led a meeting that every single person in the meeting was more qualified to lead. The eye-rolls, the whispered comments, and the overt *"Who the hell does she think she is?"* People might have laughed or simply walked out.

But not a single soldier in that room criticized me, laughed, or made a single cynical comment.

For those men and women who had served in war, they knew that the stakes are high and it might be necessary to do something with courage, outside of your skillset, experience, and comfort zone, for the good of everyone. They know that a team is only as strong as its weakest link. It's not about being the most *"experty expert"*. It's about preparation, showing up and giving your best, even when you're scared and there are few guarantees of success. That's expected from every single soldier.

As I finished the class, the older soldiers congratulated me, encouraged me, and complimented my presentation, despite the absurdity of the situation. Those are the type of people you need surrounding you. Those who will cheer you on and respect that you raised your hand, showed up, engaged in the process, and did the work, even when you weren't the most *"experty expert"*. Yet.

SUMMARY

- You don't have to be the most experty expert to add value with your perspective, taste, voice, and skill.
- The world needs more than just one person, product, or company, even if they are the best.
- Even though others are better than you, what you do still might be someone's favorite.
- Because of your price, offer, location, availability, or features, you might be the best option, even if you aren't the most experty expert.
- The world is wide enough for you and what you have to offer.
- Surround yourself with people who respect the process of showing up, trying, and growing. People who will cheer you on.

Procrastination via Preparation

"You will never plough a field if you only turn it over in your mind."
—Irish Proverb

A few years ago, in my ongoing quest for a more minimalistic life, I was sorting through old papers in a closet. Do you ever have the experience of finding something that was once so important to you, and represented so much, but at this moment in time you had nearly forgotten it? It's a confusing combination of déjà vu and nostalgia.

Picking up an old purple folder, filled with a hundred pieces of paper, I started leafing through the artifacts of an old business plan. Ten years earlier, I gave my first serious attempt at starting a business. I spent far too much money on a horrible website. I wrote out a 50+ page business plan that only my eyes ever saw. It was planned out for the next ten years of growth and expansion, every step of the way. Weeks of planning turned into months and eventually a year of planning. All the while, I never started.

Sitting on the floor, with the folder of plans never realized in hand, and knowing all I now know, a wave of emotions washed over me. Regret for never starting. Embarrassment for staying stuck for so long. Frustration—because I could have been so much farther along if I had just pivoted a bit to overcome the setbacks I faced.

Instead, I procrastinated through preparation.

Preparation felt safer and somehow more responsible. Preparation feels so productive that it eases your guilt from not starting. It seems so rational and mature.

Are You Procrastinating Through Preparation?

Here are two questions I use to gauge procrastination:

1. Have you started?
2. If so, have you hit a point where your lack of knowledge, skill set or certifications are falling short? Or do you know that you can do the work, but are constantly being asked if you have the next certification?

Sure, there are a small number of skills you need to be well into the certification process before you give it a go. Surgery comes to mind. For the 99.9% of other skill sets, we can do the work in some small way before we go *"all in"*.

Seventy-five percent of the people who I chat with who are considering getting their Certified Financial Planner (CFP) designation have never coached even a single person about money. They will say, *"Well, I'm just wondering if I should get this before I start, just in case I end up needing it."*

The hallmark sayings of those procrastinating through preparation.

"Just in case I need it."

"It could be handy to have it."

"I would feel more prepared."

Yes, by all means invest in your education, your training, your skillset. But confidence and clarity come in doing. For most of us, we also learn best while doing the thing we are trying to learn.

Study acting while acting. Study writing while writing. Learn teaching methodologies while teaching. Improve your coaching while you coach people. Up your design game while you're designing.

"But, I don't want to work in those small arenas." Sure, you'll be honing your craft in high school plays, writing an unknown blog, teaching Sunday school, coaching friends, and designing your friend's website or logo.

But remember that part about your skill set not matching your taste? It's better to practice when the stakes are lower. Practice while you learn with a warmer audience. Learn and study with fewer eyes on you.

In that business plan, I had a grand idea and a big vision for a business that never left the starting line. There were a hundred other smaller ways I could have started—small actions I could have taken. Instead I stayed stuck in preparation mode.

Mind Your Ratios

The college model is the worst example. For most people, it looks like *"spend 100% of your time learning, then when you're done here, spend 100% of your time doing."* What it lacks in effectiveness, it makes up for in simplicity. It's a very simple and efficient way to learn, at least for the college. Even though a large percentage of the population learns best by combining education with actually doing the work.

Preparation isn't a bad thing. But you need to mind your ratios.

When you start, it's fine to spend 90% of your time preparing and 10% doing. If you have ten hours a week to learn how to code, study nine hours, and practice writing code for an hour. Want to be a yoga teacher? Spend nine hours per week studying and learning, and one hour teaching (even if it's for a few friends or your kids).

Then it becomes an 80/20 ratio. Maybe you stay here for a few weeks or a few months.

70/30. 60/40. Learning, preparing, creating, and then sharing your work in an increasing proportion.

50/50. You might stay here for a year or a few years. Half of your time is preparing speeches and half is giving them.

40/60. 30/70. 20/80. You might stay here a few more years. If you have 40 hours a week, 8 hours could be spent learning, and 32 hours should be spent doing the work.

10/90. When you land here, please don't go any farther. Be a lifelong learner. Honing the craft. Studying the skill set. Always improving. If you commit to a 40 hour work week, that's four hours dedicated to learning, forever. That time is reserved for reading books, going on retreats, receiving coaching, attending conferences, listening to podcasts, or participating in classes, all designed to hone your skills. The thing you are creating and sharing is worth 10% of your time continuing to improve it.

But this chapter is about starting. Start with dedicating 10% of your time to creating and sharing. You can have 90% of your time for preparation.

Thinking back to that huge business plan in the purple folder, I still feel a lot of regret and embarrassment. But I'm also proud of that old version of myself. She was terrified and unsure, but she took a few steps. She dared to dream that she could make that business happen.

While I was sitting on the floor, flipping through the pages, I had a revelation. I couldn't believe I hadn't made the connection before. *My current work of writing about personal finance and coaching people was nearly the exact idea I had ten years earlier.* I was now doing the very thing the old version of me had set out to do. And my work now was bigger and more amazing than even those 50+ pages had contemplated way-back-when. I wish I hadn't procratisated via preparation, but I'm incredibly grateful that I found my way back to exactly where I needed to be.

SUMMARY

- Preparation is a dangerous form of procrastination because it feels so responsible and prudent.
- Ask yourself, have I started? Is this extra preparation legally necessary and are my current clients requesting or requiring it?
- Mind your ratios. Education and practice are important, but what percentage of your work week do you spend on it? As you develop skills, that percentage should continue to decrease to 90% work and 10% preparation and learning. But keep that 10% piece forever in order to keep improving.

Why not you?

"You alone are enough. You have nothing to prove to anybody."
—Maya Angelou

Just a few months into writing about personal finance, I was sitting in a coffee shop in Missoula, Montana with Ryan Nicodemus, cofounder of *The Minimalists*. We were having a coaching session and chatting about my blog.

I was explaining to Ryan that my area of personal finance was about helping people achieve more financial freedom so they could pursue work or other goals that were meaningful for them. Eventually through saving and investing, people can become Financially Independent, or FI for short, where they no longer need income from employment to pay their bills.

He looked deep in thought then said, *"Oh, it's kinda like Mr. Money Mustache? You write about things like that?"*

I felt my throat tighten up a bit and my stomach flip. He wasn't exactly wrong. Except that Mr. Money Mustache was the largest, best-known figure in my niche. Ryan was referring to the popular financial independence blog run by Pete Adeney. For many on the path to financial independence, Mr. Money

Mustache has been the introduction and inspiration for this lifestyle change. Ryan might as well have said, *"Oh, you're starting a talk show? You mean like Oprah or Ellen?"*

Mr. Money Mustache was a giant in the FI space, while I was mostly invisible.

I lowered my gaze a bit and mustered all the confidence I had to say, *"Um, yeah, I write about money in that way, like him."*

Without taking a beat Ryan said, *"Hum, he might be a good person to get to know. Maybe you can become friends with him?"*

My face turned red. It was a wave of imposter syndrome, inner criticism, and mostly embarrassment. How could I explain to Ryan that I was a no-body? That I had no place, no right, no position. I was new and invisible and insignificant.

I stared at my coffee cup and mumbled, *"Yeah, that's a good idea. Maybe."*

Everyone has a reason it shouldn't be them. A reason they don't belong. A reason they aren't good enough. A reason it couldn't work for them or they don't fit.

- You're too young or too old.
- Your ethnicity, culture, or country of origin means you'll face prejudice.
- The state, or town, or "side of the tracks" you grew up on.
- Your gender, or weight, or appearance.
- You were bullied as a kid.
- Your life has been too easy and boring.
- You weren't very good in school.
- You haven't been successful in other things.
- Your mental health challenges.
- Your learning disability.
- Your family felt dysfunctional.
- You struggle with addiction.
- You're too average.
- You're married and have kids. Or you're not married.
- You don't have connections, or money, or supportive friends.
- No one has picked you. Or believes in you.

We all have a list of reasons why we shouldn't show up, do our best work, and share that with the world.

I love watching *Comedians in Cars* and I appreciate Jerry Sienfield's occasionally non-sympathetic and straightforward perspective. A comedian will say, *"Who was I to be successful in comedy? I was just a kid from Arizona."* Almost annoyed Jerry will shoot back, *"No one cares where you're from. What does that matter? You can be funny coming from anywhere."*

Comedy seems like one of the scariest and most vulnerable ways to create work and share it with the world. As a girl from a small town in the middle of wheat fields and cattle ranches in the plains of Montana, Jerry's words are helpful for me to remember.

When a comedian says, *"Can you believe what this comic overcame. It's amazing he went through all that and still became so funny."* Jerry shoots back, *"He was probably funnier because of it."*

Why not you?

You'll need to sort through all the reasons—that never should have been reasons—that you gave for not starting or going bigger in your work.

In grade school, I almost failed first grade, and second grade, and third grade. Because of undiagnosed dyslexia, I couldn't make sense of how to organize letters and numbers. As it turns out most of first, second, and third grade is figuring out how to put those numbers and letters in the right order—something I have no talent for.

My anxiety was so bad in first grade that it made me physically ill and I missed a day of school every week.

I seemed like a very shy, not-so-bright kid who couldn't read or write.

Now I'm a public speaker, podcaster, and writer. Turns out you don't need to spell to have ideas and tell stories. There are people gifted in spelling who can help you out.

More people than I can count have told me online that I have no business writing if I can't spell. Thankfully, I had an English teacher in high school who never discounted my writing because of my spelling. I could be a writer even though I'm not a speller.

It's taken me ten years of asking, *"Why not me?"*

"Am I not hardworking? Am I not smart? Am I not kind? Am I not creative? Do I lack passion?"

I'm not everything. But I am *those* things.

We all have our reasons for holding back and we all have our challenges, but just because your path won't be identical to someone else's, doesn't mean you get nothing from your own journey.

Between having been diagnosed with bipolar disorder and raising five little kids, I'm never going to put in the 12 hour days that some of my contemporaries log regularly. I might never be as incredibly productive, but I can still have something. It might be a 12 hour week instead of a 12 hour day. But it's something.

A few years after that coffee meeting with Ryan, I met with him, and fellow podcasters Brad and Jonathan about working on an idea for a TV show.

Brad, who is a big fan of The Minimalists, asked me with a perplexed look on his face, *"How do you know Ryan?"*

Then quickly he looked like he had an epiphany, *"Of course Ryan is friends with you. You're an amazing friend. Why wouldn't someone want to be friends with you?"*

Three years after that embarrassing suggestion from Ryan about becoming friends with Pete, the man behind the Mr. Money Mustache blog, I emailed Pete. We have since met and become friends, and I asked him if he would be a speaker at my first personal finance event. Pete happily agreed to attend, as his way of showing his support for my work.

Your inner critic will create lots of reasons you can't do the work you really care about.

These reasons you *"can't"* are more accurately labeled the reasons *"it will take more work"*, *"you'll have slower progress"*, or *"you'll not be at the absolute top."* But these aren't reasons for not starting.

Start where you need to start. Be yourself. Be okay with imperfect progress. Accept that it may take far longer than you would like to get where you want to go.

We all have to pay the price of admission to do the work we love. Your price might be higher than what others have to pay. Maybe unfairly high. You might have a mountain of challenges compared to mountains of opportunity that others seem to have at their disposal.

When I look back at those mountains and challenges that I had to overcome, while others smoothly sailed by, I try to set my mind on a different perspective. Those mountains helped me become a mountain climber. They taught me that I can do hard things and I can endure discomfort, fear, and even suffering. I don't identify with all the ways life has knocked me down. Instead I focus on the idea that *I am the rising*.

A few years ago, I was being interviewed by a grad student for a research paper. Somehow we started talking about the profound impact Oprah's work has had on my life trajectory when I was young and more recently on my work. She laughed and said almost off-handedly, *"Wouldn't it be cool if you met her someday?"*

I must have missed the part where she was joking because I said matter of fact, *"Well, of course it'll happen. It's just a matter of time."*

Her laughter became nervous because of my certainty.

Without thinking, I said *"Oh honey, you have no idea how far I've already come. I've walked a thousand miles to get to this point. Meeting Oprah is just a little farther up the road."*

Maybe it takes writing 20 more books. Maybe it takes 30 years. But why not me?

Why not you?

SUMMARY

- Everyone has reasons and insecurities that make them feel unqualified or that their goals are impossible.
- Those reasons might make progress slow or imperfect. But there's no reason not to start.
- The cost of admission might be high. But you can do hard things.
- Ask, *"why not you?"*

A Small Request....

If you have enjoyed this book so far, would you mind leaving a review on Amazon? My goal is for this book to be the essential guidebook for every creative or entrepreneur who shares their work online. Positive reviews on Amazon go a long way to helping more people discover these ideas.

PART 3

··

Failure, Fear, and Finding the Courage to Share Your Best Work

Courage and Dedication.

Courage is stepping into something that might not work. Dedication is taking that step over and over again.

I'm always delighted to meet the newbies and *"next-levelers"* in any field. I have incredible admiration for these people. Because I think they are the most courageous and dedicated among us.

You can be the most courageous because what you create and share probably won't work. Not the first time at least. But you keep trying anyway. That takes nerve and guts.

You can be the most dedicated because you show up every day. You don't have the momentum created by past successes to push your work along. Everything you create takes effort and commitment as you push that rock up the hill.

You might not have enormous talent, or huge victories, just yet. But courage and dedication is all you need to start new ventures or to move in new directions.

Part 3 of this book is about how to stay in the game. How to keep going when things don't break your way. And when the shit hits the fan and the whole Internet turns on you, you'll learn how to manage those storms that can last days, if not months.

As Simon Sinek teaches: this isn't a finite game, it's an *infinite game*. To stay in the game forever, you have to curate who gets a seat at the table to give you feedback and criticism. And who gets voting rights in your work. You'll need to be able to move through the feelings of failure. You'll find safer places to anchor your professional identity, like in your actions and process, so the wins and losses don't blow you about.

Cancel Culture

*"You turning off your own TV isn't censorship. You're trying
to get other people to turn off their TV because you don't
like something they're watching, that's different."*
—Ricky Gervais

The term *"cancel culture"* is thrown around a lot, but what is it really? I think the confusion and often misuse of the idea creates a lot of unnecessary fear for new creatives and entrepreneurs. The fear is that you can do something that's not wrong, but perceived by some to be wrong and then have your whole career unjustly taken from you. But that is the extreme exception in cancel culture, not the rule.

In the next chapter, we'll chat about how to handle making a public mistake. Or options if you are incorrectly thought to have made a mistake. But first let's chat about what this thing we call *"cancel culture"* really is.

I see three levels of criticism or accountability that happens in that we tend to label cancel culture.

Your Audience is Mad

I have a habit of quoting TV shows or movies randomly in my writing, often left unattributed as a sort of Easter Egg for other die hard fans to appreciate. I once titled an email *"Boats! Boats! Boats!"* and received a landslide of delighted emails from fans of *"How I Met Your Mother."*

I try to write to my email list as though we are lifelong friends simply chatting about things. Most of the time this works out just fine, and occasionally I get myself in trouble. Because, in fact, we are new acquaintances on the Internet.

One of my all time favorite movies is a 90's romcom with Meg Ryan titled *French Kiss.* In her adorable way she was ranting about the French man who stole her suitcase and her cheating fiance said with disgust *"All men are bastards."* Without any context, I added that to an email.

And then I experienced my all time largest unsubscribe percentage of any email I've ever sent. I apologized in the next email to everyone who stuck around. Of course, all the people who unsubscribed never saw that apology or explanation.

Was I canceled? No. I offended a bunch of people and they left, which they have every right to do. Sometimes you will mess up and there are consequences for those actions. Sometimes people will just figure out that you, your product or company isn't to their liking.

I'm not a perfect, polished, or god-like influencer. I'm messy, and fully human, and have bad days, and am a trying-to-figure-it-all-out kind of content creator. Some people want a model of perfection to aspire to—a guru or zen master.

I can honestly say I gave *"perfection"* an incredibly dedicated attempt for years. Always trying to do everything right, please everyone, and hit the mark. If it would have been possible, I would have achieved it. Instead, for all that effort, I had a mental breakdown, addiction struggles and chronic pain. So when I decided to create content online, I made a deal with myself that I would only create if I was allowed to be fully human. The trade off is that I'm not for everyone. That's a trade-off I'll happily take.

It's okay when people or customers leave. They probably weren't the ones for you anyway.

Random Haters Show Up

The second stage is where random critics and haters arrive on your platforms or create brand new content, like news articles, to criticize you. Maybe it's because you made a mistake, weren't to their liking or they find your actions offensive.

It can create a big dust storm. If you don't believe you've done anything wrong, my advice would be to take a break from the Internet and let it blow over. Especially if 95% of the people making a fuss aren't your fans or customers and instead are people who simply like to make a fuss online. Let them make a fuss. They would never have been your fan or customer anyway. Your true fans will probably go to bat defending you on your behalf. I get it, it feels awful at the moment. But the random strangers will get distracted by the next thing that irritates them soon enough.

Bully Others

These random haters might form a campaign against you in an attempt to bully, shame or persuade your fans to leave you. They might take it a step further and try to get companies, brands or employers to disengage from you.

When you feel you haven't done anything wrong, this is a powerless and unfair spot to be. Sometimes the line between accountability and unfair punishment is unclear or there isn't much consensus about it.

It would be easier if things were black and white. If I murdered someone, there would be some consequences to that. I imagine some companies wouldn't want to engage with my brand, on account of the murdering.

If you ever find yourself in a spot where you feel canceled, there are a few options. First, there are less single entry gatekeepers left. If you lose one job, one sponsor, one deal, there are often others out there.

Second, you have to mess up really badly to get banned from the Internet. Even if a large percentage of the world wishes you were canceled, you still get to exist.

Third, despite the haters' efforts to convince others to hate you, your fans will make up their own mind. In some ways it's easier to convince a company to drop you than a fan. Your job is to connect and serve your customers and audience. And if you can do that effectively, we arrive at option number four.

Which is that most companies are profit-minded. If you have a base of customers and fans, and you need a company to partner with you, you'll probably find one eventually.

The greatest risk of cancel culture is that in the storm, you become so discouraged and defeated that you decide to take your ball and go home.

SUMMARY

- Sometimes people will disapprove or decide your brand or product isn't to their liking and leave, which is fine.
- Sometimes they will gather a mob of critics and haters to stir up a sandstorm online.
- In the worst cases, you will lose work and income opportunities because a mob convinces companies to drop you.
- It's hard to be canceled forever if you don't quit. So instead continue to show up and serve your fans and customers.

When it Hits the Fan

"Success is not final, failure is not fatal: it is the courage to continue that counts."
—Winston Churchhill

onvertKit is an email provider geared towards creators. I've been a fan and customer for years, but a few years ago they made a very public mistake. The company had a huge rebrand in the works for months. A new name, logo, colors, website, everything was changing. But when it was previewed to users, a significant percentage of their customers were hurt and offended by the new name due to cultural appropriation.

The mark of a great company isn't in never making a mistake. A company and founder's character and wisdom are tested in the response. ConvertKit's response was so spot on that instead of diminishing my respect for the company, it increased it.

When it Hits the Fan

Two things can cause the proverbial *"crap"* to hit the fan. Either you did something wrong, and it feels like the entire Internet is angry about it—OR—the entire Internet *thinks* you did something wrong, and they are angry about it.

There is a chance you might escape this. Your company, brand, product, or ideas might go decades with a squeaky-clean reputation. Never making a misstep. So the Internet might never fully turn on you.

In the last ten years, I've only experienced isolated incidents online. I have watched this experience unfold with others in much more severe cases, either involving professional friends or observing from farther away with bigger brands, celebrities, and companies.

There seems to be a helpful way to handle it and an unhelpful way to respond. In this chapter, I'm going to try to outline the helpful way.

When You're Wrong

Ultimately, behind every product, platform, idea, and company are people. These people sometimes make mistakes, and you will make mistakes, too. There are times that you were trying to do the right thing, but it came out the wrong way. Perhaps you gave your best and it just wasn't good enough or it wasn't what the audience wanted. After the fact, with the angry crowds of Internet strangers and fans chanting, you realize that you were wrong.

Here is a road map out.

Step 1: Take a breath

Take an hour. Go for a walk. Take a day. Turn off the Internet. Put your phone in a cupboard. Stop reading comments and checking DMs. Connect back to real life. Connect to your body, to nature, to other in-person friends and family.

Same for your team or your company. Take a one-hour outdoor picnic lunch with no talk of work.

People will rage even more that you aren't there to fight in real-time. They will up their game trying to bait you and egg you on. They will be outraged that you have the audacity to go for a walk while they are trying to burn you down.

Do it anyway.

You responding to their franticness with your own frantic energy will only amp up the chaos.

If it's a Facebook group that's imploding or a social media channel going sideways, and you need more than an hour to address the problem, explain you need to take a day to pause and reflect. Say something like, *"I see and hear these concerns, and because it matters to me/us/our company so much, we are going to take some time to listen and hear and think so we can come back to the conversation with better understanding."*

Step 2: Listen and Understand

Sometimes we know exactly what we did wrong. But often, when we make a misstep unknowingly, and the Internet breaks, we need to understand others' points of view.

After you have taken your breath, it's time to listen.

ConvertKit did this brilliantly. They listened.

For weeks they requested emails and had conversations with customers who voiced their grievances. They called customers. They video chatted with them. Why did the new name upset them? What did the name mean to them in their culture and religion? How was it inappropriate as a company name?

I've watched content creators rush to offer an apology without really seeking to understand the problem. It's a shortcut to ease the current discomfort. But your audience will see straight through it. It's one thing to put out a placeholder apology with the understanding that there is an ongoing information gathering process happening. But you can't sweep it under the rug to avoid doing the real work.

After weeks of listening and understanding, ConvertKit then continued on to step 3.

Step 3: Apologize

I've never been good at apologizing. Ask anyone who knew me in my 20's; I was basically allergic to it. I used to feel bad that I was so deficient in this.

It turns out most people in the public eye are. But I'm also proof that it's a learnable skill.

After high school, I attended Bible College for a year. One of the most helpful concepts I learned there was *"Take total ownership in any problem for your own percentage. If you were 10% wrong and the other person 90% wrong, you need to take 100% ownership for your 10% wrong."*

You might only be 10% wrong. 100% own up to that 10%. 100% apologize for that 10%.

An honest, accountable apology is so rare that it almost always feels refreshing. Especially when it comes early, not after the trial is over. Once you fully understand what you did wrong and how it impacted people, stating that as clearly and plainly as you can goes a long way. It's like throwing a bucket of ice water on the fire. You get a little smoke, but the fire is basically gone. The fastest way to take the wind out of someone's argument is to acknowledge, take ownership, and apologize in a complete and up-front way.

Step 4: Fix. Repair. Make changes going forward.

"Here's how we are changing this going forward."

For some people, words may be enough. But a lot of people want to see action and lasting change. Actions prove that you are serious. Money talks too. I see a lot of companies throw money at outside organizations to attempt to fix a situation, but I feel like it carries more weight if you commit money internally to finding lasting solutions.

In the summer of 2020, during protests, riots, and the Black Lives Matter movement gaining more momentum, many companies gave donations to organizations dedicated to equality. Which would have been nice, except, employees in those companies pointed out the lack of equality and opportunity in their own organization. Make sure your own house is in order.

Optional Step: Over-Communicate

In some situations, where there are complex things happening in the company, you need to communicate that—frequently, to the point where it even may appear to be a bit redundant. When I interviewed Jason Fiefer from *Entrepreneur*

Magazine, he said that one of the biggest mistakes companies can make is under-communicating. Or even worse, not communicating information and updates at all—to both internal and external stakeholders. Your employees and customers should never learn about how things are unfolding in your company from outside news sources. They should hear it—frequently and proactively—from you.

Transparency is key while the problems are sorted through.

Under Attack but not Wrong

It's hard when we make public mistakes and need to clean up and repair. But there is one thing worse—when you're under attack, but you haven't done anything wrong.

I've seen this play out in two ways:

Sorry, Not Sorry

One of the most heartfelt examples of this was after Christy Teigen, a supermodel and cookbook author, shared the story of her miscarriage on Instagram along with images of her and her husband grieving in the hospital. During this time of immense pain, she also faced backlash for sharing such a personal and intimate moment.

Her response in the op-ed piece she wrote and posted on her Instagram boiled down to a simple idea. *It's my life, my story, and this is what I wanted to capture and share. If you don't like it, it's not for you. Sorry, but I'm not sorry.*

There will be times that a large percentage of Internet strangers, fans, and even customers will strongly disagree with you. But if you're not wrong, you're not wrong.

Jen Hatmaker, a prolific author and popular online presence had an enormous fan base of faith-centered women. When she came out in support of gay rights, equality, and a safe home for LGBTQ people within faith communities, a large swath of dedicated fans and readers were outraged. This wasn't a 48-hour controversy. Hate, anger, and long-winded comments rolled in for months. It was a long burn, and as an outsider, the amount of anger she received was horrifying.

And she didn't back down. Not once. Not for a second. Instead, she kept boldly affirming what she believed to be true. She was empathetic and kind, yet unflinching. I'm not sure many people who were angry *"got over it."* A large swath of her audience who disagreed with her left for good, and a whole new group of people who appreciated her LGBTQ support joined.

I'll Prove It

The other approach I see people and organizations take is, *"I'm not wrong, and I'll prove it."* Occasionally, the thing you are accused of can be shown to be incorrect.

This is different from engaging in the fight and scrambling to defend yourself in every comment. It's like the process above, but instead of the apology, it reads, *"This is what we/I am accused of. And I agree if that were the case, it's a serious thing. But in this case, it's not true."* And if possible, you show evidence otherwise.

Some people won't believe you. Some people will want to hate you, anyway. That's their choice.

A conference I regularly attend came under fire for paying women and people of color significantly less than their white male counterparts for speaking engagements. It was a serious accusation, attendees and sponsors alike were very concerned about it. So the event formed a committee of well-known attendees, opened their financial books, and cleared the air. With action and transparency, they were able to regain their credibility and trust with most people.

An End in Sight

At some point, there is a chance you'll have to weather some variation of this storm. Maybe it's just a stormy night. Maybe it's a hurricane. Maybe it's a wildfire that burns for months.

But you will come through it. Eventually. Even Monica Lewinsky, who arguably has faced one of the worst media storms of my lifetime, has found peace on the other side of the storm.

SUMMARY

- If you or your company made a mistake: take a breath, listen and understand, apologize, fix and repair the damage. And if applicable, over-communicate.
- If you are in the storm but not wrong you can take a strong stand with *"sorry, not sorry."* Or prove the accusations against you are false.

Optimize for not Quitting

"There's one thing you need to optimize for when you're starting a project. Not quitting."
—Bryan Harris

My first consistent writing was about mental health. After years of avoiding my own emotions, trauma, and ignoring the mental health symptoms I had experienced since I was a teenager, the inevitable happened. I had a mental breakdown. Breakdown is probably too charitable of a word to describe what happened. Breakdown sounds like a car pulled over on the side of the road with smoke wisping out from under the hood, the owner impatiently waiting on a tow truck. Trainwreck is a more accurate metaphor for what happened to me when things unravelled.

I completed a month-long stay at a treatment facility and left with the understanding I was going to have to start feeling my feelings and learn to manage this thing I knew nothing about called bipolar disorder. Overwhelmed, terrified, and a little pissed off, I decided to start writing. Over the next two years a friend and I wrote about managing bipolar on our blog. We didn't care if it didn't become a big thing. We weren't really sure if we actually wanted other people to read it.

We wrote to process the grief, the joy and the confusion that bipolar, medication, mania, therapy, and depression had all created. We wrote out the conversations and thoughts we couldn't bear to say out loud. And that was exactly what we needed.

Fast forward a few years, and a lot had changed. I stopped writing after my son passed away unexpectedly. Words, stories, and ideas escaped me for some time. My husband and I went on to adopt a sibling group of three. Then we had another biological child. We bought our first home with cash. Bought rental properties. We were able to become financially independent, meaning that our investments and passive income could cover all of our expenses, indefinitely.

I had taken an interest in personal finance when I was 19. Newly married with $55,000 of debt and working in a low-paying career, I knew I wanted more choices and options than I had growing up near the poverty line. So I started reading books. Over 500 non-fiction books in the first ten years alone. I took classes about money and personal finance.

But something changed inside me with that bipolar diagnosis. My husband and I had been saving and investing 50% of our income since we married. Maybe it was the grief, maybe it was fear, or maybe I correctly assessed the situation: I wasn't going to be cut out for a 40 hour workweek, working 50 weeks a year. So we started on this path of financial independence. All together, it took thirteen years to go from $55,000 in debt to financial independence at age 32.

The year I reached financial independence, I hatched a plan to take a year off. I framed it as an experiment—a *"mini-retirement"*— to test out this idea of not working a *"normal"* job. I had the freedom and flexibility to give it a go.

I wrote out a long list of what we wanted to do in our year off: Fix up our master bathroom, take a six week trip with the kids, and many other items on our to-do list. And after a long absence from writing, I jotted on the list *"something to do with writing."*

I didn't really care that almost no one read my first blog. I wanted to write about the challenges that accompany a bipolar diagnosis simply as part of my own healing—having other people read it was secondary.

But this new project? I wanted to write about personal finance to help other people figure out their money so they could have more freedom and choices.

More options. Maybe like me, others wanted more time with their kids, to travel and explore, and to pursue *"passion projects."* In short, I wanted other people to read what I wrote so it could be helpful to them. I wasn't just writing for myself anymore. Even though I couldn't quite figure out how to achieve it, I wanted this project to be both impactful and profitable.

This project had stakes. It mattered. But the number one thing to optimize for is not quitting.

Figure Out the Worst Case Scenario

> *"Fear Setting is a way to visualize all the bad things that could happen to you, so you become less afraid of taking action."*
> —Tim Ferriss

My youngest was just a few weeks old when I started this project. I would sit in a big chair in my bedroom feeding him and map out all the things I would write about.

I had the fear almost all of us have before we start. *"What if no one reads it? What if no one cares? Or no one likes it?"* Given the readership of my other blog, this wasn't an entirely unfounded concern.

What was the worst case scenario? The conversation in my head followed the script of the chat God had in the desert with Abraham. Abraham asks if God would spare the city of Sodom and Gomorrah if 100 righteous people lived there? What if it's only 50? Only 20? Only 10?

"Would I write this blog if only 100 people read it?
Yes.
What if only 50 people read?
Yes, for 50 I'll write.
What if only 20 people read?
For 20, I'll write.
What about 10 people?
No, I'm not writing for only 10 people."

In the end I settled for 15 people. If 15 people would read, I would continue to maintain my blog.

Fifteen people was my worst case scenario. It wasn't my ideal number of readers, but I had committed to not quitting as long as there were 15 people.

In incredible luck, the curator for a huge personal finance site loved a preview I sent him. He featured one of my posts the first day I published, sending thousands of people to my blog. I had found my 15.

When you find your worst case scenario, you can look it square in the face and figure out how you'll deal with it. How can you solve it? What will be the back up plan? How can you get out of the situation?

Once you see the problem clearly, the solution becomes more clear. *"What if my content isn't popular?"* wasn't specific enough. In part, because that's a benchmark that will always move. Fifteen people was a problem I felt confident I could solve.

And if you're wondering, it was also my worst case scenario for this book. I won't write it if only two or three people read it. But I'll write it for 15 people. That's a challenge I know I can rise to.

Create a Wide Circle

Some problems, like finding 15 readers, you know you can overcome. Then there are some problems that when you look them square in the face, you know they will crush you. If that worst case scenario happens, you're done.

At one of my many 9-5 jobs I had before I embarked on this creative, entrepreneurial life, I had one particularly bad day at work.

Through a series of unfortunate events, none of which made sense at the time, I had managed to piss off about 50% of my coworkers. I'm used to not being everyone's cup of tea, but in general I'm fairly well liked and easy to get along with. Having people being honest-to-goodness angry with me was horrible.

To make matters worse, the issue at hand poked at an old trauma of mine, so I was a mess. For the first and only time in my working life, I found myself crying in the bathroom.

On this very bad, no-good day at work, one of my family members walked into my place of work. They heard about how bad of a day I was having and decided to stop by. In an incredibly naive moment, a bubble of hope for comfort and support rose up inside me. I have never so horribly misread a situation.

For the next 20 minutes, my family member berated me, yelled at me, and shamed me. The main theme was, *"See, now everyone knows what I have always known; you're a horrible person. You should be fired. You disgust me."* This was all said in front of all of my coworkers, some customers, and really anyone who cared to listen in. I just stood there—shocked and humiliated with tears rolling down my face.

Maya Angelou said *"When people show you who they are, believe them the first time."* This wasn't the first time I had been shown how my family member would treat me, but this time I believed what they showed me.

When I started creating things and actively sharing them online, I knew I would have bad days. Days where I misspoke or made mistakes. Days when the Internet turned against me. Days with comments from harsh critics and huge failures for everyone to witness. Using all the things we talk about in this book, I thought I could survive that. I optimized well enough that I wouldn't quit.

But on those few exceptional *"no good"* days, I knew what could sink the ship: criticism from certain people in my family. And I knew how far they would go to sink me. While humiliation was the *"tactic of the day"* used on me that fateful day at work, it was only one of the sinking tactics I had experienced over the years.

So how do you optimize for not quitting when you're dealing with an unfixable problem?

Create a wide circle about it. Create a buffer—and maintain it.

For me, I didn't tell a soul in my family what I was doing. I wrote anonymously. I didn't use my first name or last name. I didn't use my picture. My website had a random name instead of jillianjohnsrud.com which it is now.

Sure, there were lots of people in my family who would have been incredibly supportive and wonderful about my work. But it wasn't worth the risk. So I stayed anonymous for two years. Once I got to the point where I felt strong and confident enough in my work to handle Internet strangers hating me and a few family members piling on the hate as well, I started sharing my name, my pictures, and changed my website to my full name.

Until I felt that I was strong enough to withstand criticism from my inner circle, I maintained a wide circle of anonymity around my work, buffering me from the force of potential blows that I knew could be strong enough to cause me to quit.

It's okay to avoid the thing that might cause you to quit. Especially at first.

If Twitter makes you want to quit, then quit Twitter instead. If unsupportive opinions from old friends might cause you to quit, don't tell them. If your website is so frustrating it might cause you to quit, hire someone else to design it.

The number one thing to optimize for is not quitting.

"If I don't...."

"If I don't..." happens in our own mind. It's a game we create for ourselves. A game you have a good chance of losing. I call it the *"If I don't..."* game.

The *"If I don't..."* game sounds like this:

If I don't...
- Earn $40,000 my first year
- Sell 10,000 units
- Grow my online presence to 30,000
- Get this big contract
- Score a big job this first year
- Go full time in the next two years
- Get 5,000 subscribers my first year

That means I...
- Am not cut out for this.
- Don't have what it takes.
- Won't be successful.
- Can't make it work.
- Should quit.
- Am no good.

The *"If I don't..."* game is win or lose. And you usually put the stakes just close enough to the edge that there is a good chance you'll lose.

If you want to optimize for not quitting, don't stack the game against you. If you have to play this game, rig it so you always win!

Ideally, you play a game of process <u>not</u> outcomes. For example, *"I'm going to write every week, and that means I'm a writer." "I'm going to keep baking and sharing my work online and that means I'm committed to my craft."*

Second best is a game of process <u>and</u> outcomes. *"I'm going to write every week because I'm a writer. I'm sharing that work to grow my audience, because I know as soon as my audience is large enough I can get a book deal."*

"I'll keep working and growing my business on the side. As soon as my side gig covers my bills and I have a two year emergency fund, I'll commit full time to my side business, making it my main thing, and quit my 9-5 job."

If you are going to play the game of outcomes, make them ones you can absolutely crush. Like finding 15 people to read this book.

These small, easy goals don't have to be the end goal. It's great to have big audacious goals to inspire you. But also create micro goals. Little stepping stone goals. The ones that show you that you're moving in the right direction.

While I might start with 15 readers, one day, I'd love 50,000. Speaking of which, you should probably recommend this book to a few friends. It's better to read it as a group anyways.

SUMMARY

- The most important thing to optimize for is not quitting.
- Use Fear Setting to follow your worst case scenarios to the very end.
- Problem solve or create a wide circle to avoid the thing that will make you quit.
- Manage your own expectations and disappointments by creating micro goals.

Test and Scale.
Don't "Go Big or Go Home"

"Great things are not done by impulse, but by a
series of small things brought together."
—Vincent Van Gogh

After one of my podcast interviews, I was catching up with my guests, Bryce and Kristy, who are published authors. Knowing that I was working on this book, they had some very good questions for me. *"Have you started on a proposal? Are you talking to agents? What kind of publisher are you thinking about?"*

I said, *"Right now, my goals are to get started. And write."*

Those are important questions, but I knew trying to figure it all out would overwhelm me. Getting started and doing the work were big enough goals for me to tackle first. You don't need to plan out 27 steps ahead. Not only is it near impossible, but it's likely to get you stuck.

That's Go Big or Go Home thinking.

Go Big or Go Home (GBGH) is perfectly crafting the journey from start to finish. It's waiting for the perfect time where everything comes together. It's making a big gamble or taking a huge risk.

That 50+ page plan for my first business in the purple folder was an example of Go Big or Go Home thinking. It was a perfectly crafted plan spanning years into the future before I took a single step. It was an attempt to build something perfectly without first engaging in the process of doing the work.

Nine out of ten times, GBGH is a train wreck. You'll crash and burn. You might manage to dust yourself off and try GBGH a few more times. Soon enough, you will take your ball and go home, burned, bitter, and disillusioned with the whole thing. Convinced the game is for suckers or the few lucky ones.

You don't need a grand gesture. You just need to start.

You don't need to quit your job or to take out a huge loan to get started. Just sit down and do the work that needs to get done to accomplish the first few small steps. Feel the sense of accomplishment, and let that be your fuel to accomplish more and more small steps going forward—one foot after the other—every day.

The truest path to success is the one where you learn as you go. It's nimble and flexible. It adjusts with new information and inputs. It's a constant experiment and making micro pivots. This path is focused on big picture outcomes, but is adaptive on the journey.

The process of *"Test and Scale"* involves asking the question: *"What can I do in 1 to 4 hours that would move the ball down the field?"* What would be a small test, conversation or action step to help you learn something needed to achieve the larger goal?

If your test focuses on personal growth or relationships, even better. Learn a skill, information, or something about yourself. Connect with other people who are connected to your goals.

I started writing this book at arguably the worst possible time—summer of 2020. My kids had been home for months, we were trying to homeschool, I couldn't leave the house. Oh, and just for fun, we were moving into one of our rental houses that we are in the process of renovating.

So I started with the smallest viable option. Every morning I jotted down a few thoughts on a post-it note. I didn't have hours to write—let alone form coherent sentences, paragraphs or chapters.

Perfectionists like me get stuck here. We want a perfect plan before we really start: which is procrastination via preparation. We want to be totally confident in the end destination before we begin—despite the fact that confidence and clarity come by doing. We want what we create to be at least as good as the best out there, even though our skill does not yet match our taste. So we end up getting stuck at the starting line.

I constantly have to remind myself that to get something great, you have to sit in the messiness of iterations. Nothing starts fully baked or fully formed. It's in the process of improvement that something becomes great. Ford Motor Company didn't start with today's version of the company. Google didn't start out as it is today. There is no amount of preparation or luck that will let you start at the end. You only get to cross the finish line by starting and improving as you go.

Even if all you have time and bandwidth for is one sentence on a Post-It note, that's enough. Don't wait for the perfect time or perfect plan to Go Big or Go Home. Just start. Share. Then keep going.

SUMMARY

- Go Big or Go Home (GBGH) thinking causes you to try to create the perfect plan, at the perfect time with every detail figured out before you even start. And it almost never works.
- Test and Scale starts with a step you can take in 1 to 4 hours. Ask a question, have a conversation, research one bit of information, fill out one form.
- Each test gives you the feedback, information and growth you need to know how to make a micro pivot before your next 1 to 4 hour test.
- No amount of preparation or luck will let you start at the finish line.

Create Emotional Boundaries from the Outcomes You Seek

"I have already settled it for myself, so flattery and criticism go down the same drain and I am quite free."
—Georgia O'Keeffe

We live in a culture driven by outcomes. Even more unhelpful is the culture of caring about a single metric of an outcome that you are trying to achieve. When people ask how your diet is going, what are they really asking? What's the only metric they appear to care about: did you lose weight?

But there are a lot of data points you could measure. Did you try new healthy foods that you liked? Did you learn how to cook some new recipes? Did you figure out how to make more healthy choices when eating out? Did you break your soda habit? Did you find an exercise you enjoy and can do almost every day?

Those other metrics probably matter a whole lot more in the long run to your weight loss success. You could go on a crash diet of lemon juice and maple syrup and lose weight, but that's neither sustainable nor healthy.

That's why you need to create some emotional boundaries from the outcomes that you are working towards. If you did all the right things to lose weight but the numbers on the scale didn't move you might think, *"I'm a loser. I'll never get this right. What's the point?"* That's crazy talk, right? You're still better off by practicing the habit of eating healthy and exercising even if the scale doesn't budge right away.

It's also crazy to tie your identity to your professional outcomes. Many professional outcomes depend on events or decisions that are not in your control. You can do everything right and miss one metric. Or you can be successful in one metric, but not be set up for long-term success. Hitching your identity to specific outcomes creates a rollercoaster of emotions that won't serve you well in the long term.

Your Work Stands Alone

Just like in the children's song, *"Farmer in the Dell,"* at the end the cheese stands alone. Your work also stands alone. Like we talked about in Part One, once it's shipped out into the word, it's grown. Let your work, work. If it stirs people up, creates a ruckus, and some people who you didn't make the work for hate it, that's fine. Your work is grown.

But if your work wins or loses, it also stands alone.

Your personal identity needs healthy boundaries from the outcomes of your work.

I find it funny when people praise certain celebrities as being *"down-to-earth"* or *"so relatable"*. Because the assumption is that a person's work success will mix with their personal identity and will cause them to become weird, unrelatable or self-obsessed. Or if their latest professional work is not well-received and tanks, it should also tank their personal life right along with it.

We talked about how you aren't your work. It lives separately from you. You also aren't your work's wins or losses. You live separately from the outcomes.

I know for the *"Enneagram three"* or achievers among us, this seems like an impossible distinction, but bear with me.

If you entangle your personal identity with work outcomes, your personal life loses either way. If your work wins, you run the risk of becoming a self-absorbed, arrogant weirdo. Your work doing reasonably well may cause you to mistakenly believe that other aspects of your life must also be going well. In reality, we all know someone who bankrupted their personal life or sacrificed their health so that their work could be successful.

If your work loses, you might also mistakenly feel as if your whole life is falling apart and actually trash the best aspects of your personal life in the process.

Untangle that idea.

De-couple your personal identity and the totality of your life from professional outcomes that you don't fully control in the first place.

Intention, Not Identity

I care very much about my work outcome. I put so much intention, time, energy, and love into helping my work have good outcomes. I'm invested in my work's outcome. It matters a lot.

And I'm still not the outcome. I'm still just me.

You can care about the outcome and still create a healthy boundary between your identity and the outcome of your work.

My Work Did That

I remember when in the tiniest corner of the Internet, my work started becoming *"Internet famous."* I would meet fans of my work at events, and they would tell me how my work has had a deep impact on their lives.

But as we talked about before, often fans want the work to be the person and the person to be the work. So these people would act like they were big fans of me and that I, personally, had deeply impacted their life.

I'm incredibly grateful that my work went out into the world and made such a significant difference in their life. But that wasn't me creating that impact or outcome. I was chilling at home in Montana, making pancakes or sitting by the river.

I had no idea how to handle these kinds of interactions with fans, who were so often mixing my identity in with my work's outcomes. There was a lot of crying and hugging and incredibly flattering things said to me, but it always made me nervous.

I felt out of my depth navigating these interactions and it was causing me a ton of anxiety. I was at an event with my friend Paula Pant, who is a dream at handling this type of attention from people who had been impacted by her work. When interacting with her excited fans, she is like David Grohl of the Foo Fighters—effortlessly cool, confident and funny. She handles the spotlight like a true rockstar, while I freeze like a deer in the headlights: awkward, sweaty, and terrified to let people down.

I finally asked her, *"How do you manage those conversations so well? After the initial gushing and the tears, I'm not really sure where to take the conversation with a fan of my work."*

She said, *"Oh, that's easy. Take the attention away from you and just bring it back to the work. Ask your fan a question about the event. Ask them if they have a favorite piece that you wrote? Whether this is their first time at this event, or what talks have they enjoyed the most?"*

It takes practice. Practice in how you mentally view your work as something separate from you. Then start practicing the language you will use when you think and talk about your work. The ninja level is achieved when you subtly bring the conversation and the credit away from you and back onto the work, where it rightly belongs.

Last year after I finished speaking at an event, I lingered by the stage and chatted with several of the other speakers. I spotted a young woman coming toward us, her face full of fear and on the verge of tears. I could spot her nervous and excited energy even from 50 feet away. As soon as she started talking, the tears started flowing.

"I just needed to tell you that you changed my life. I took your free course and you saved my marriage, transformed our finances, and you helped me find my faith again."

I gave her a quick hug, *"I'm so happy to hear that my work was helpful for you changing your life. It sounds like you really put in the hard work! Congratulations. That's wonderful."*

I'm so incredibly thankful that my work had an impact. So grateful. But "I" did not change her life, save a marriage, or save her faith. She did that work. My work was only a helpful catalyst.

Falsely assuming I did any of those things would only turn me into a weirdo and be very challenging for my mental health. I created the work. The work went out into the world fully grown and did it's job.

You're not your work. Your work stands alone if it wins or loses.

You get to have a rich, vibrant personal life, no matter what mischief your work is up to.

SUMMARY

- There is always more than one metric to measure in each outcome.
- You can do everything right and still not have the ideal outcome.
- Mixing your identity with your work's success can turn you into an arrogant jerk.
- Mixing your identity with your work's failures can be devastating at a personal level.
- Untangle your work and its outcomes from your identity.
- Be careful about the language you use with yourself and others about you versus your work. You are not your work.

Actions and Voting Members

"Success means doing the best we can with what we have. Success is the doing, not the getting; in the trying, not the triumph."
—Zig Ziglar

A few months after I started writing about personal finance, there was a big conference for personal finance content creators called FinCon. Several thousand people would be there—writers, podcasters, YouTubers, and financial companies. I really wanted to attend but I was also at the tail end of breastfeeding my youngest. I knew if I went to the event, even being as prepared as I could be, it would also mark the end of this special season with my baby. Sorting through feelings of loss at missing the event, I realized the part of the event I was most looking forward to was strengthening and building relationships.

I knew my intention was to build relationships with my new tribe of creatives and entrepreneurs. Just because the event wasn't going to work out didn't mean I couldn't take a different approach to engage this community.

I spent the next year discovering and testing new ways to connect and build relationships within the financial independence community. I left comments on other people's blogs and websites, interacted with them on social media, sent emails, set up video chats, organized group video discussions, and spent time with them on the phone.

The next year, at the event, I signed in to get my name tag and as I walked away from the registration table someone I knew from my online relationship-building efforts spotted me. I stood there for hours talking to person after person. After seeing over 50 online friends in person for the first time, I headed off for the first opening keynote.

We often pin too much hope on getting the one big break that will open everything up for us. In reality, it's showing up consistently and taking the right steps that get us where we want to go. If you stay in the game long enough, do the work long enough, it's entirely likely that at least a few breaks will come your way.

I have a large supportive community of creatives and entrepreneurs, not because I went to the right event, happend to sit at the right table, or was invited to the right party. It's because I showed up for people and engaged and supported them when it mattered, over and over and over.

Actions Create Identity

In the creative and entrepreneurial life there aren't many firm spots you can tether your ship. You can't trust public opinion. One day the masses will love you, and the next day people will be death-threat-level angry. Or the masses will totally ignore you until after your death, like the Vincent Van Goghs of the world. Public opinion is no place to anchor your identity, self-worth, or even to reliably gauge the impact of your work.

You shouldn't be like a ship that is adrift, subject to being continually tossed about, at the mercy of online haters, your inner critic, the wins and losses or even the lucky breaks.

There are two firm anchors to which you can tether your boat

1. Your actions create your identity; and
2. Who gets a vote.

In his great book, *Atomic Habits,* James Clear talks about how identity-based habits are more effective, impactful, and ultimately can be more permanent.

I believe that our actions can help form our sense of identity. If you write everyday, you start to feel like a writer. You start to believe that you are a writer. If a book sells well or not, if you get a book deal or not, if you have all five star reviews or only a few three star reviews, it's the daily writing habit that anchors your identity. You're a writer because you write.

How do I know I'm not a tennis player? I don't play tennis. Ever.

I won't try to untangle the personal and spiritual implications. Suffice it to say that for your professional life, your professional actions can become your professional identity. However you act, that's what you get to be.

If your actions are consistently kind, you get to be kind. If your actions are honest, you get to be honest. If you work hard, you're a hard worker. If you act like an asshole, you get to be an asshole.

When the haters hate, you get to keep your actions.

When your inner critic comes out in full force, take her to task. Does that criticism hold up 100% of the time with your actions? If she wails, *"I'm not a writer! I'll never be a writer!",* you can point out the fact that you are writing and sharing that work everyday. You might not be an amazing writer, a well-known writer, an award-winning writer, but you are in fact a writer.

When you don't get the outcome you want, you have your actions. If you did the work, if you followed the process, if you gave 100%, that's good enough. Next time will be better.

Who Gets A Vote

The second anchor is knowing who gets a vote. Brené Brown says she keeps a small piece of paper in her wallet with the names of everyone whose opinion of her actually matters to her. And it's a very short list.

I think about it like being in a boardroom. Who gets a seat at the table? Who's opinions and thoughts are considered. Who do you go to for advice, as a sounding board? Who will you take feedback and corrections from?

Who are your voting board members? When it comes down to it, who makes the call? Whose votes are considered? In my work, I hold about 50% of the voting rights. Most of the time I make the final call. But if all other voting members and all other people I turn to for advice (*"board members"*) are dead set for or against something, I listen to the people I have chosen to trust.

While writing this book, I had to make a hard call on the budget. It threw me out of sorts. I immediately reached out to about five people who I wanted to have a seat at the table. I wanted their advice and opinions. Ultimately my husband and I were the only voting members. We carefully considered everyone's thoughts and advice, and then we made the call.

Your *"board"* and your voting members can't be the entirety of the Internet. It should be a short list. Have a small group of people that you can bring questions or challenges to. People who know you, who you trust, and who like you. Give them a seat at your table. They can examine your intent and your actions. They can speak into your life. Then ask voting members to vote with the benefit of this broader perspective.

Sometimes you'll make the wrong decision or cast your vote against the good advice you received. Maybe you'll need to apologize or make amends. Sometimes things won't break your way, and you'll have to pick yourself up and dust yourself off.

Either way, tomorrow is a new day and another opportunity to do the right thing.

You get up and you do the work. Then you share that work, your very best that is within you with the world.

SUMMARY

- Don't count on lucky breaks, commit to the actions.
- Let your actions be a tether of your identity.
- Choose who gets to speak into your life and who gets a vote.
- Regardless of the outcome, keep going. Sit down and do the work—every day.

Ch 23

Trust the Process

"We can trust the practice. We can acknowledge that future outcomes are uncertain, but remind ourselves that our process is all we've got."
—Seth Godin

One of the most powerful and impactful things a teacher ever said to me could have been misconstrued as an insult.

When I was about 17, my math teacher Mr. Melhoff mentioned to the class a bet of sorts he had made with another teacher about who would be the best female basketball player in our school. The bet had been made years earlier when I was in Jr. High.

He told the class he had bet on me. Then he kind of shrugged and said, *"I guess I was wrong on that one."*

I felt a little wave of embarrassment and anxiety as everyone in the class looked at me. They knew he was right. I wasn't anywhere near the best basketball player in the school.

I'm not sure if he sensed the tension in the room or was just continuing his thought, but he added, speaking directly to me, *"The reason I bet on you was you outworked every other girl. You were here early in the morning before school, shooting hoops. And late in the evenings, when I drove out of the parking lot, you were still out there practicing. All on your own. No one was prompting you or even paying attention. And that's what it takes to be the best."*

I never became a great basketball player and was far from the best. But I felt extremely seen and validated for those years where I had put in all of those hours, all on my own, never realising that someone had noticed.

Even though I didn't get the outcome I wanted in basketball, Mr. Melhoff's off-hand compliment caused me to never doubt the process again. If everyday I worked with courage and dedication, everyday I put in the work, leaned into uncertainty and vulnerability, showed up when no one was looking and trusted the process, then maybe someday I would alchemize a bit of talent and luck from all of that work.

You can't trust the haters or the trolls, you can't trust the nagging voice of imposter syndrome, you can't trust the unearned confidence (or doubt) of your family and friends, you can't even trust the outcomes—but you can trust the process.

I've never been in a room where I was the most talented, or the smartest, or the best educated, or the most charismatic. But I've been in a few rooms where my work was the star. Everyone carefully listened to what I had to say. For no other reason than the years I spent leaning into the work, trusting the process, and growing as a person while no one was watching or paying any attention.

Mr. Melhoff was right, *"That's what it takes to be the best."*

⬤ Resources

Everyone, at some point in their life, should do work that they are passionate about. Something they love, that matches their interests, skill set, and creates positive change in the world. Maybe it grows into a multi-million dollar business. Maybe it is able to pay all of your bills. Or maybe it barely helps pay the cost of creating and sharing it with the world.

After we deal with the fear of Internet critics, imposter syndrome, opinions of friends or family and dealing with failure, one big issue often remains:

"I can't afford to..."

- Pay for the initial investment.
- Take the time off.
- Pay your bills while you do this work.
- Deal with the financial setbacks and failures that happen along the way.

I know that dealing with money, budgets and investing can feel boring. But nothing will be more high leverage in advancing your creative and entrepreneurial work than figuring the money stuff out.

Getting good with money will help you create a safety net to handle the inevitable setbacks. And you can build a financial runway, to buy yourself a few months or even a few years to figure out how to grow your business and make it profitable.

Figuring out your finances gives you options: the freedom, time and the confidence to simply explore new things.

At *jillianjohnsrud.com/money* I share ten ways you can start figuring out your finances, so instead of it being a stumbling block to your creative and entrepreneurial dreams, it can become the accelerator.

Free Courses

Set Up Your Platform

For those who are ready to start sharing your work online, first things first, let's set up your platform. Tech stuff can be frustrating and overwhelming. It was for me when I started! So I have created a set of videos that walks you through every click and step (with written instructions!)

You'll learn how to get a domain, set up your website, create an easy and beautiful design and start growing your email list….in less than an hour!

https://www.jillianjohnsrud.com/platform/

Ramp Up Your Content Strategy

Every type of business that wants to connect with people online needs a content strategy! No matter if you are selling custom mugs, a hair stylist or a writer. In this free video course + workbook, you'll create a content strategy that will allow you to find, connect with and convert your customers. From a social media plan to the SEO on your website, this short course will take less than an hour to finish but will save you years of spinning your wheels without any real growth.

https://www.jillianjohnsrud.com/content/

All Free Course + Resources

I'm always creating resources to help people create more financial freedom empowering them to design meaningful and enjoyable lives. Get access to all my free courses here.

https://www.jillianjohnsrud.com/free/

References

Barry, Nathan. "There and back again; the story of renaming CovertKit", Nathan Barry, 4 August 2020, https://nathanbarry.com/rename/.

Below, Brittanni. "Living Brave with Brene Brown and Oprah Winfrey", YouTube, 4 November 2017, 20:45, https://www.youtube.com/watch?v=JmCjExkFz4Q.

Ferriss, Tim. "Fear-Setting: The Most Valuable Exercise I Do Every Month", The Tim Ferriss Show, 15 May 2017, https://tim.blog/2017/05/15/fear-setting/.

Flynn, Pat. Personal Interview. Everyday Courage Podcast September 2021

Jimmy Kimmel Live. "Celebrities Read Mean Tweets #10", YouTube, 21 September 2016, 3:04, https://www.youtube.com/watch?v=JgQVj4iMm8Y.

Morrison, Toni (@ToniMorrison). "If there's a book you want to read, but it hasn't been written yet, then you must write it." Twitter, 30 October 2013, https://twitter.com/ToniMorrrison/status/395708227888771072.

Podrazik, Joan. "Oprah's Life Lesson from Maya Angelou: 'When People Show You Who They Are, Believe Them'", HuffPost, 14 March 2013, https://www.huffpost.com/entry/oprah-life-lesson-maya-angelou_n_2869235.

Simon, Samantha. "25 Stars Who Suffer from Imposter Syndrome", InStyle, 8 December 2017, https://www.instyle.com/celebrity/stars-imposter-syndrome.

Sinek, Simon. "The Infinite Game: How to Lead in the 21st Century", YouTube, 13 May 2019, 1:31:19, https://www.youtube.com/watch?v=3vX2iVIJMFQ.

TheEllenShow. "Ellen's First Monologue of Season 18", YouTube, 21 September 2020, 7:01, https://www.youtube.com/watch?v=Egn3CuQRHW8&t=1s.

Acknowledgments

In sitting down to write this acknowledgements page, I wished there were more places in life to put an acknowledgements page. I could have written one with every job or promotion I received, when my family grew, at anniversaries and accomplishments. It seems a shame to only have them published in books, music albums or given as short speeches during awards ceremonies. Because we all have far too many people to acknowledge and be grateful for. It's another compelling reason for me to write lots and lots of books.

But since this is my first book, I have some catching up to do.

My mom. In a world that felt chaotic and scary to me growing up, she was steady. She is a rock and tether, a friendly and safe harbor.

My great grandparents, Doris and Charlie, were my cozy, soft place to hide and grow and explore.

And my hometown, Big Sandy, Montana. It's a place coursing with hard work, grit and the pursuit of excellence. I honestly don't think I would have become the same person if I grew up anywhere else. The school staff, neighbors and friends hold a dear place in my heart.

Writing a book seems simple enough. Sit down and type and gather all those ideas together. In reality it was like a complex set of gears twirling, all working together and playing a role. The sitting down and typing bit is just one part. And in some ways the easy part.

The idea to write this book started with my clients and friends. The ideas were born and worked out in conversations full of honesty and vulnerability. I know the challenges so intimately, not just from having experienced them, but because I heard them from you, my readers, in dozens and dozens of conversations. It allowed me to find solutions that worked for all of us.

My incredible audience of email subscribers, you are like sunshine to a young plant. For reasons I still don't exactly understand, you show up each week and welcome me. You engage with my stories, my ideas and my life. And allow me into yours. When the Internet seems a strange and scary place, you reveal the beauty of a community choosing to grow together.

Then there were all the hands that helped move the book forward. My coach and dearest friend, Nick True. My publishing guru, M.K. Williams who pulled me out of the mud dozens and dozens of times over the year-long journey. My beta readers, especially Peter Gallant who offered over a thousand notes. My writing buddy August. I wanted to write this book like I would chat with a friend, so I imagined I was simply writing out an email to you. Our weekly chats helped me organize the ideas and inspire the topics covered in this book. My editor, Tabitha, whose passion for spelling and grammar mirrors my indifference for those things. And everyone on my team who makes the company run while I hide away and write books.

And most of all my husband, Adam. I could write an entire book about how you have chosen to love me. Your passion and dedication for making my dreams a possibility is a gift I can never repay, but will always strive towards.

And to my children, for all the interruptions, distractions, laughter and hugs. I might have become a very serious and boring person if not for your constant fart jokes.

About the Author

Jillian has been slowly growing her creative and entrepreneurial life since she was a teenager. About once a month she realizes she's not cut out for this life and quits, but only for a few hours.

Her work has been featured in Forbes, Good Morning America, USA Today, Glamour, and Parents. Her work has been viewed over a million times with it's fair share of praise and criticism.

She is a popular podcast guest, speaker and coach. She runs an online education company teaching people how to create financial freedom while building meaningful and enjoyable lives.

Over the last 19 years of marriage, she and her husband, Adam, have adopted 4 kids, had 2 biological kids, traveled to 40+ of the United States and 27 more countries, lived abroad, bought and renovated homes, then became financially independent in their 30s.

Jillian and Adam live in Montana with their 5 kids and dog, Cheesy Taco. They spend their time reading, hiking, drinking tea, watching their ducks and traveling with their kids.

You can connect with Jillian on social @jillianjohnsrud if you have something nice to say. Or for speaking and interview requests email her at jillianjohnsrud@gmail.com

Made in the USA
Las Vegas, NV
26 November 2022

60368833R00099